D0013127

MASTERY

MASTERY

The Keys to Long-Term Success and Fulfillment

George Leonard

A DUTTON BOOK

DUTTON
Published by the Penguin Group
Penguin Books USA Inc., 375 Hudson Street,
New York, New York 10014, U.S.A.
Penguin Books Ltd, 27 Wrights Lane, London W8 5TZ, England
Penguin Books Australia Ltd, Ringwood, Victoria, Australia
Penguin Books Canada Ltd, 2801 John Street,
Markham, Ontario, Canada L3R 1B4
Penguin Books (N.Z.) Ltd, 182–190 Wairau Road,
Auckland 10, New Zealand

Penguin Books Ltd, Registered Offices:
Harmondsworth, Middlesex, England

First published by Dutton, an imprint of New American Library,
a division of Penguin Books USA Inc.
Distributed in Canada by McClelland & Stewart Inc.

First Printing, February, 1991
10 9 8 7 6 5 4 3 2 1

 REGISTERED TRADEMARK—MARCA REGISTRADA

Library of Congress Cataloging-in-Publication Data
Leonard, George Burr, 1923–
    Mastery : the keys to long-term success and fulfillment / George
Leonard.
        p. cm.
    1. Success. 2. Self-realization. I. Title.
    BF637.S8L445 1991
    158′.1—dc20   90–46343
                                                   CIP

Printed in the United States of America
Set in Garamond Light
Designed by Eve L. Kirch

For John and Julia Poppy

CONTENTS

ACKNOWLEDGMENTS

Heartfelt appreciation goes to *Esquire*'s editor emeritus Phillip Moffitt for his wise counsel and generous support, and for his empassioned and enduring advocacy of this book; he speaks with the authority of one who is himself on the path of mastery.

I owe a great deal to my aikido teachers, Frank Doran, Robert Nadeau, and Bill Witt, and especially to Nadeau, who introduced me to the idea of presenting exercises based on aikido principles to a wider, non–martial arts constituency. Richard Strozzi Heckler, Wendy Palmer, and I have been doing aikido together for eighteen years—first as students, then as teachers and co-owners of Aikido of Tamalpais: But we are more than fellow martial artists, for our lives touch in many ways; Richard and Wendy are part of this book. Annie Styron Leonard has once again been a loving critic and a perceptive editor.

Thanks to master tennis teacher Pat Blaskower for

her eloquence on the particulars of the mastery process, as presented in Chapter One, and to Joe Flower, who conducted interviews on the subject of mastery with leading sports figures. I'm grateful, as always, to Sterling Lord, an intrepid pathfinder for twenty-five years.

A special word of thanks goes to John and Julia Poppy, to whom this book is dedicated. John and I have been colleagues and friends for twenty-eight years—at *Look* magazine, at *Esquire*, and actually in all things. He has contributed immeasurably to each of the Ultimate Fitness features, bringing a rare intelligence, elegance, and clarity to the most difficult subjects. The light that is Julia Poppy, my sister, has illuminated my path for a lifetime, and her spirit has touched everything I've done. This book would not be possible without them both.

INTRODUCTION

In 1987, for the fourth straight year, the May issue of *Esquire* magazine featured a special section on what it called Ultimate Fitness. These special sections claimed a broader charter than is usual for such a subject. "Ultimately," I wrote in the first of the series, "fitness and health are related to everything we do, think and feel. Thus . . . what we are calling Ultimate Fitness has less to do with running a 2:30 marathon than with living a good life."

The previous Ultimate Fitness specials had enjoyed exceptionally high reader interest, but the May 1987 number was something else again. The subject this time was mastery, "the mysterious process during which what is at first difficult becomes progressively easier and more pleasurable through practice." The purpose of the feature was to describe the path that best led to mastery, not just in sports but in all of life, and to warn against the prevailing bottom-line mentality that puts quick, easy results ahead of long-term dedication to the journey itself.

The response was immediate and extravagant. Requests for extra copies, tearsheets, and reprints poured in. Management newsletters requested permission to reprint portions of the *Esquire* feature. Corporate CEOs gave photocopies to their officers. Training groups of a wide variety spent hours discussing the mastery principles. Letters to the editor were numerous and eloquent. A navy carrier pilot, for instance, wrote that he had been having trouble landing the F-14 Tomcat on an aircraft carrier. "I . . . was in the process of making a second and perhaps final attempt when I bought the May issue. Insights that I gained from Mr. Leonard's outline of the master's journey gave me the extra 10 percent of mental discipline that I needed to make the trek down this portion of my path a relatively easy one."

I knew a book was needed to provide a full understanding of how to get on and stay on the path of mastery, but at the time, I was working on a memoir of the 1960s. I thought interest in the subject might wane, but it hasn't. The many comments and inquiries that I continue to receive have convinced me more than ever that the quick-fix, fast-temporary-relief, bottom-line mentality doesn't work in the long run, and is eventually destructive to the individual and the society. If there is any sure route to success and fulfillment in life, it is to be found in the long-term, essentially goalless process of mastery. This is true, it appears, in personal as well as professional life, in economics as well as ice skating, in medicine as well as martial arts.

It was the martial arts, in fact, that gave me the original idea for the *Esquire* feature and for this book. I have practiced aikido since 1970, and have taught it regularly since 1976. With its sophisticated blending moves and full repertory of rolls and falls, aikido is generally known as the most difficult of the martial arts to master. On the training mat, every attempt at circumvention or overreaching is revealed; flaws are made manifest; the quick fix is impossible. At the same time, the pleasures of practice are intensified. The mat, I often tell my students, is the world, but it is the world under a magnifying glass.

An aikido school is therefore an ideal laboratory for studying the factors that work for and against long-term learning. As hundreds of students passed through our school, I began to recognize distinctive patterns in the way they approached the art. The types of learners I would later characterize as the dabbler, the obsessive, and the hacker (see Chapter Two) revealed themselves, in most cases, after only a few classes. I was surprised to discover that it wasn't necessarily the most talented who would persevere on the long road to black belt and beyond. I began to realize that although different people might take different paths to mastery, all of the paths led in the same general direction—one that could be clearly mapped.

But would my findings at the aikido school apply to other skills? Interviews conducted at the time of the *Esquire* special and since then, along with the extraordinary response to the magazine feature itself, have shown me that what is true for aikidoists is also true for learners in any nontrivial skill: managers, artists, pilots, schoolchildren, college students, carpenters, athletes, parents, religious devotees, and even entire cultures in the process of change.

Bottom-line thinking might now prevail, but the master's journey has deep roots. It also has deep resonance. One might say, in fact, that it's not so much an idea whose time has come as an idea that has always been with us—it's just that we need to be reminded. I'm pleased that so many people's lives have already been changed for the better through this reminder, and I hope the book will add to the number of those who are on the path.

 **PART ONE**

THE MASTER'S JOURNEY

Introduction

Start with something simple. Try touching your forehead with your hand.

Ah, that's easy, automatic. Nothing to it. But there was a time when you were as far removed from the mastery of that simple skill as a nonpianist is from playing a Beethoven sonata.

First, you had to learn to control the movements of your hands (you were just a baby then) and somehow get them to move where you wanted them to. You had to develop some sort of kinesthetic "image" of your body so that you could know the relationship between your forehead and other parts of your body. You had to learn to match this image with the visual image of an adult's body. You had to learn how to mimic your mother's actions. Momentous stuff, make no mistake about it. And we haven't yet considered the matter of language—learning to decode sounds shaped as words and to match them to our own actions.

Only after all this could you play the learning game that parents everywhere play with their children: "Where's your nose? Where are your ears? Where's your forehead?" As with all significant learning, this learning was measured not in a straight line but in stages: brief spurts of progress separated by periods during which you seemed to be getting nowhere.

Still, you learned an essential skill. What's more important, you learned about learning. You started with something difficult and made it easy and pleasurable through instruction and practice. You took a master's journey. And if you could learn to touch your forehead, you can learn to play a Beethoven sonata or fly a jet plane, to be a better manager or improve your relationships. Our current society works in many ways to lead us astray, but the path of mastery is always there, waiting for us.

Chapter 1

What Is Mastery?

It resists definition yet can be instantly recognized. It comes in many varieties, yet follows certain unchanging laws. It brings rich rewards, yet is not really a goal or a destination but rather a process, a journey. We call this journey *mastery,* and tend to assume that it requires a special ticket available only to those born with exceptional abilities. But mastery isn't reserved for the supertalented or even for those who are fortunate enough to have gotten an early start. It's available to anyone who is willing to get on the path and stay on it—regardless of age, sex, or previous experience.

The trouble is that we have few, if any, maps to guide us on the journey or even to show us how to find the path. The modern world, in fact, can be viewed as a prodigious conspiracy against mastery. We're continually bombarded with promises of immediate gratification, instant success, and fast, temporary relief, all of which lead in exactly the wrong direction. Later, we'll take a look at the quick-fix, antimastery mentality that pervades our society, and see how it not only prevents us from developing our potential skills but threatens our health, education, career, relationships, and perhaps even our national economic viability. But first let's examine mastery itself.

The master's journey can begin whenever you decide to learn any new skill—how to touch-type, how to cook, how to become a lawyer or doctor or accountant. But it achieves a special poignancy, a quality akin to poetry or drama, in the field of sports, where muscles, mind, and spirit come together in graceful and purposive movements through time and space. Sports provide a good starting point for this exploration, in that results of training in the physical realm are rather quickly and clearly visible. So let's take a familiar sport, tennis, as a hypothetical case through which we can derive the principles underlying the mastery of all skills, physical or otherwise.

Say you're in fairly good physical shape but by no means a highly conditioned, skilled athlete. You've played around with movement sports such as volleyball and softball, which involve hand-eye coordination, and you've played a little tennis, but not much—which might be a good thing. If you're going to go for mastery, it's better to start with a clean slate rather than have to unlearn bad habits you picked up while hacking around. Now you've found a teacher, a pro with a reputation for grounding players in the fundamentals, and you've committed yourself to at least three visits a week to the tennis court. You're on the path to mastery.

It starts with baby steps. The teacher shows you how to hold the racket so that it will hit the ball at the correct moment in time. She has you bring the racket forward in a forehand swing until you find the position of maximum strength of the wrist. She stands in front of you on the same side of the net and tosses balls to your forehand, and after each hit, she asks you to tell her if you hit it early or late. She shows you how to move your shoulders and hips together with the motion of the arm, and to stride into the ball. She makes corrections, gives encouragement. You feel terribly clumsy and disjointed. You have to *think* to keep the parts of your body synchronized, and thinking gets in the way of graceful, spontaneous movement.

You find yourself becoming impatient. You were hoping to get exercise, but this practice doesn't give you enough even to break a sweat. You like to see the ball go across the net and into the dark green part of the court, but your teacher says you shouldn't even be thinking about that at this stage. You're the type of person who cares a lot about results, and you seem to be getting hardly any results at all. The practice just goes on and on: hold the racket correctly; know where the racket makes contact with the ball; move shoulders, hips, and arm together; stride into the ball—you seem to be getting exactly nowhere.

Then, after about five weeks of frustration, a light goes on. The various components of the tennis stroke begin to come together, almost as if your muscles *know* what they should do; you don't have to think about every little thing. In your conscious awareness, there's more room to see the ball, to meet it cleanly in a stroke that starts low and ends high. You feel the itch to hit the ball harder, to start playing competitively.

No chance. Until now your teacher has been feeding balls to you. You haven't had to move. But now you're going to have to learn to move side to side, back and forth, and on the diagonal, and then set up and swing. Again, you feel clumsy, disjointed. You're dismayed to find that you're losing some of what you'd gained. Just before you're ready to call it quits, you stop getting worse. But you're not getting any better, either. Days and weeks pass with no apparent progress. There you are on that damned plateau.

For most people brought up in this society, the plateau can be a form of purgatory. It triggers disowned emotions. It flushes out hidden motivations.

You realize you came to tennis not only to get exercise but also to look good, to play with your friends, to *beat* your friends. You decide to have a talk with your teacher. How long, you ask, will it take you to master this thing?

Your instructor responds, "Do you mean how long would it take for you to automatically get into position and hit a forehand effectively to a target?"

"Yes."

She pauses. It's a question she always dreads. "Well, for someone like you, who starts tennis as an adult, if you practice an hour three times a week, it would take, on average, five years."

Five years! Your heart sinks.

"Ideally, about half of that would be instruction. Of course, if you're particularly motivated, it could be less than that."

You decide to try another question. "How long will it be before I can play competitively?"

"Competitively? That's a loaded term."

"I mean playing to try to beat a friend."

"I would say you could probably start playing after about six months. But you shouldn't start playing with winning as a major consideration until you have reasonable control of forehand, backhand, and serve. And that would be about a year or a year and a half."

Another bitter dose of reality.

The teacher goes on to explain. The problem with

tennis isn't just that the ball moves and the racket moves, and you have to master all of that, but also that *you* have to move. In addition, unless you're hitting with a pro who can put the ball in the correct place, a lot of practice time on the court is spent picking up balls. Backboards are helpful. Ball machines are helpful. But playing for points, trying to beat a friend, really comes down to who gets the serve in the court and who misses the ball first. Points last only about three hits over the net. You don't get much practice. What you really need is to hit thousands of balls under fairly controlled circumstances at every step along the way: forehand, backhand, footwork, serve, spin, net play, placement, strategy. And the process is generally incremental. You can't skip stages. You can't really work on strategy, for example, until you've got placement pretty well under control. With the introduction of each new stage, you're going to have to start *thinking* again, which means things will temporarily fall apart.

The truth begins to sink in. Going for mastery in this sport isn't going to bring you the quick rewards you had hoped for. There's a seemingly endless road ahead of you with numerous setbacks along the way and—most important—plenty of time on the plateau, where long hours of diligent practice gain you no apparent progress at all. Not a happy situation for one who is highly goal-oriented.

You realize that you have a decision to make at some point along the journey, if not now. You're tempted to drop tennis and go out looking for another, easier sport. Or you might try twice as hard, insist on extra lessons, practice day and night. Or you could quit your lessons and take whatever you've learned out on the court; you could forget about improving your game and just have fun with friends who don't play much better than you. Of course, you could also do what your teachers suggests, and stay on the long road to mastery. What will you choose?

This question, this moment of choice, comes up countless times in each of our lives, not just about tennis or some other sport, but about everything that has to do with learning, development, change. Sometimes we choose after careful deliberation, but frequently the choice is careless—a barely conscious one. Seduced by the siren song of a consumerist, quick-fix society, we sometimes choose a course of action that brings only the illusion of accomplishment, the shadow of satisfaction. And sometimes, knowing little or nothing about the process that leads to mastery, we don't even realize a choice is being offered. Yet even our failures to choose consciously operate as choices, adding to or subtracting from the amount of our potential that we will eventually realize.

The evidence is clear: all of us who are born without serious genetic defects are born geniuses. Without an iota of formal instruction, we can master the overarching symbolic system of spoken language—and not just one language but several. We can decipher the complex code of facial expressions—a feat to paralyze the circuitry of even the most powerful computer. We can decode and in one way or another express the subtleties of emotional nuance. Even without formal schooling, we can make associations, create abstract categories, and construct meaningful hierarchies. What's more, we can invent things never before seen, ask questions never before asked, and seek answers from out beyond the stars. Unlike computers, we can fall in love.

What we call intelligence comes in many varieties. Howard Gardner of Harvard University and the Boston University School of Medicine has identified seven of them: linguistic, musical, logical/mathematical, spatial, bodily/kinesthetic, and two types of personal intelligences that might be described as intrapersonal and interpersonal. We vary in our giftedness in these seven at least. Still, each of us comes equipped with enough raw ability across the board to achieve that seemingly rare and mysterious state we call mastery in some mode of thought and expression, some interpersonal and entrepreneurial enterprise, some art or craft.

This is also true in the physical realm. It was once believed that our primitive ancestors were rather pitiable creatures compared with the other animals of the jungles and savannahs. Lacking the fangs, claws, and specialized physical abilities of the predators, our forefathers supposedly prevailed only because of their large brains and their ability to use tools. This supposition has downplayed the prodigious human ability to create complex, well-knit social groupings, a challenge which, more than toolmaking, accounts for the development of the large brain.

It also downplays the human body.

Much has been made of the blazing sprint-speed of the cheetah, the prodigious leaps of the kangaroo, the underwater skills of the dolphin, and the gymnastic prowess of the chimpanzee. But the fact of the matter is that no animal can match the human animal in all-around athletic ability. If we were to hold a mammal decathlon with events in sprinting, endurance running, long jumping, high jumping, swimming, deep diving, gymnastics, striking, kicking, and burrowing, other animals would win most of the individual events. But a well-trained human would come up with the best overall score. And in one event—endurance running—the human would outperform all other animals of comparable size, as well as some quite a bit larger. If we are born geniuses of thought and feeling, we are also geniuses *in potentia* of the body, and there is undoubtedly some sport, some physical pursuit in which each of us can excel.

But genius, no matter how bright, will come to naught or swiftly burn out if you don't choose the master's journey. This journey will take you along a path that is both arduous and exhilarating. It will bring you unexpected heartaches and unexpected rewards, and you will never reach a final destination. (It would be a paltry skill indeed that could be finally, completely mastered.) You'll probably end up learning as much about yourself as about the skill you're pursuing. And although you'll often be surprised at what and how you learn, your progress towards mastery will almost always take on a characteristic rhythm that looks something like this:

The Mastery Curve

There's really no way around it. Learning any new skill involves relatively brief spurts of progress, each of which is followed by a slight decline to a plateau somewhat higher in most cases than that which preceded it. The curve above is necessarily idealized. In the actual learning experience, progress is less regular; the upward spurts vary; the plateaus have their own dips and rises along the way. But the general progression is almost always the same. To take the master's journey, you have to practice diligently, striving to hone your skills, to attain new levels of competence. But while doing so—and this is the inexorable fact of the journey—you also have to be willing to spend most of your time on a plateau, to keep practicing even when you seem to be getting nowhere.

Why does learning take place in spurts? Why can't we make steady upward progress on our way toward mastery? As we saw in the case of tennis, we have to keep practicing an unfamiliar movement again and again until we "get it in the muscle memory" or "program it into the autopilot." The specific mechanism through which this takes place is not completely known, but it probably matches up fairly well with these informal descriptions. Karl Pribram, professor of neuroscience and a pioneering brain researcher at Stanford University, explains it in terms of hypothetical brain-body systems. He starts with a "habitual behavior system" that operates at a level deeper than conscious thought. This system involves the reflex circuit in the spinal cord as well as in various parts of the brain to which it is connected. This habitual system makes it possible for you to do things—return a scorching tennis serve, play a guitar chord, ask directions in a new language—without worrying just *how* you do them. When you start to learn a new skill, however, you do have to think about it, and you have to make an effort to replace old patterns of sensing, movement, and cognition with new.

This brings into play what might be called a cognitive system, associated with the habitual system, and an effort system, associated with the hippocampus (situated at the base of the brain). The cognitive and effort systems become subsets of the habitual system long enough to modify it, to teach it a new behavior. To put it another way, the cognitive and effort systems "click into" the habitual system and reprogram it. When the job is done, both systems withdraw. Then you don't have to stop and think about, say, the right grip every time you shift your racket.

In this light, you can see that those upward surges on the mastery curve are by no means the only time anything significant or exciting is happening. Learning generally occurs in stages. A stage ends when the habitual system has been programmed to the new task, and the cognitive and effort systems have withdrawn. This means you can perform the task without making a special effort to think of its separate parts. At this point, there's an apparent spurt of learning. *But this learning has been going on all along.*

How do you best move toward mastery? To put it simply, you practice diligently, but you practice primarily *for the sake of the practice itself.* Rather than being frustrated while on the plateau, you learn to appreciate and enjoy it just as much as you do the upward surges.

But learning to love the plateau is getting ahead of our story. First, let's meet three characters—the Dabbler, the Obsessive, and the Hacker—who go through life, each in his or her own way, choosing *not* to take the master's journey. Who knows?—we might be meeting ourselves.

 Chapter 2

Meet the Dabbler, the Obsessive, and the Hacker

We all aspire to mastery, but the path is always long and sometimes rocky, and it promises no quick and easy payoffs. So we look for other paths, each of which attracts a certain type of person. Can you recognize yourself in any of the following three graphs?

The Dabbler

The Dabbler approaches each new sport, career opportunity, or relationship with enormous enthusiasm. He or she loves the rituals involved in getting

19

started, the spiffy equipment, the lingo, the shine of *newness*.

When he makes his first spurt of progress in a new sport, for example, the Dabbler is overjoyed. He demonstrates his form to family, friends, and people he meets on the street. He can't wait for the next lesson. The falloff from his first peak comes as a shock. The plateau that follows is unacceptable if not incomprehensible. His enthusiasm quickly wanes. He starts missing lessons. His mind fills up with rationalizations. This really isn't the right sport for him. It's too competitive, noncompetitive, aggressive, nonaggressive, boring, dangerous, whatever. He tells everyone that it just doesn't fulfill his unique needs. Starting another sport gives the Dabbler a chance to replay the scenario of starting up. Maybe he'll make it to the second plateau this time, maybe not. Then it's on to something else.

The same thing applies to a career. The Dabbler loves new jobs, new offices, new colleagues. He sees opportunities at every turn. He salivates over projected earnings. He delights in signs of progress, each of which he reports to his family and friends. *Uh oh*, there's that plateau again. Maybe this job isn't right for him after all. It's time to start looking around. The Dabbler has a long resume.

In love relationships (perhaps an unexpected place to look for the signs of mastery, but a good one), the

Dabbler specializes in honeymoons. He revels in seduction and surrender, the telling of life stories, the display of love's tricks and trappings: the ego on parade. When the initial ardor starts to cool, he starts looking around. To stay on the path of mastery would mean changing himself. How much easier it is to jump into another bed and start the process all over again. The Dabbler might think of himself as an adventurer, a connoisseur of novelty, but he's probably closer to being what Carl Jung calls the *puer aeternus,* the eternal kid. Though partners change, he or she stays just the same.

The Obsessive

The Obsessive is a bottom-line type of person, not one to settle for second best. He or she knows results are what count, and it doesn't matter how you get them, just so you get them fast. In fact, he wants to get the stroke just right during the very first lesson. He stays after class talking to the instructor. He asks what books and tapes he can buy to help him make progress faster. (He leans toward the listener when he talks. His energy is up front when he walks.)

The Obsessive starts out by making robust progress. His first spurt is just what he expected. But when he inevitably regresses and finds himself on a plateau, he simply won't accept it. He redoubles his effort. He pushes himself mercilessly. He refuses to accept his boss's and colleagues' counsel of moderation. He works all night at the office, he's tempted to take shortcuts for the sake of quick results.

American corporate managers by and large have joined the cult of the bottom line; their profile is often that of the Obsessive. They strive mightily to keep the profit curve angled upward, even if that means sacrificing research and development, long-term planning, patient product development, and plant investment.

In relationships, the Obsessive lives for the upward surge, the swelling background music, the trip to the stars. He's not like the Dabbler. When ardor cools, he doesn't look elsewhere. He tries to keep the starship going by every means at his command: extravagant gifts, erotic escalation, melodramatic rendezvous. He doesn't understand the necessity for periods of development on the plateau. The relationship becomes a rollercoaster ride, with stormy separations and passionate reconciliations. The inevitable breakup involves a great deal of pain for both partners, with very little in the way of learning or self-development to show for it.

Somehow, in whatever he is doing, the Obsessive manages for a while to keep making brief spurts of upward progress, followed by sharp declines—a jagged ride toward a sure fall. When the fall occurs, the Obsessive is likely to get hurt. And so are friends, colleagues, stockholders, and lovers.

The Hacker

The Hacker has a different attitude. After sort of getting the hang of a thing, he or she is willing to stay on the plateau indefinitely. He doesn't mind skipping stages essential to the development of mastery if he can just go out and hack around with fellow hackers. He's the physician or teacher who doesn't bother going to professional meetings, the tennis player who develops a solid forehand and figures he can make do with a ragged backhand. At work, he does only enough to get by, leaves on time or early, takes every break, talks instead of doing his job, and wonders why he doesn't get promoted.

The Hacker looks at marriage or living together not

as an opportunity for learning and development, but as a comfortable refuge from the uncertainties of the outside world. He or she is willing to settle for static monogamy, an arrangement in which both partners have clearly defined and unchanging roles, and in which marriage is primarily an economic and domestic institution. This traditional arrangement sometimes works well enough, but in today's world two partners are rarely willing to live indefinitely on an unchanging plateau. When your tennis partner starts improving his or her game and you don't, the game eventually breaks up. The same thing applies to relationships.

The categories are obviously not quite this neat. You can be a Dabbler in love and a master in art. You can be on the path of mastery on your job and a Hacker on the golf course—or vice versa. Even in the same field, you can be sometimes on the path of mastery, sometimes an Obsessive, and so on. But the basic patterns tend to prevail, both reflecting and shaping your performance, your character, your destiny.

At some of my lectures and workshop sessions, I describe the Master, the Dabbler, the Obsessive, and the Hacker. I then ask the people in the audience to indicate by a show of hands (leaving the Master out) which of the other three would best describe themselves. In almost every case, the response breaks down into nearly even thirds, and the discussion that follows shows how easily most people can identify with the three types who are the subject of this chapter.

These characters, then, have proven useful in helping us see why we're *not* on the path of mastery. But the real point is to get on that path and start moving. The first challenge we'll meet, as we'll see in the next chapter, is posed by our society.

Chapter 3

America's War Against Mastery

If you're planning to embark on a master's journey, you might find yourself bucking current trends in American life. Our hyped-up consumerist society is engaged, in fact, in an all-out war on mastery. We see this most plainly in our value system. Values were once inculcated through the extended family, tribal or village elders, sports and games, the apprenticeship system or traditional schooling, religious training and practice, and spiritual and secular ceremony. With the weakening or withering away of most of these agencies, value-giving in America has taken a strange new turn.

Our society is now organized around an economic system that seemingly demands a continuing high level of consumer spending. We are offered an unprecedented number of choices as to how we spend our money. We have to have food, clothing, housing, transportation, and medical care, but within certain limits we can choose among many alternatives. We are also enticed by a dazzling array of appealing nonnecessities—VCRs, vacation cruises, speedboats, microwave ovens. Every time we spend money, we make a statement about what we value; there's no clearer or more direct indication. Thus, all inducements to spend money—print advertisements, radio and television commercials, mailers, and the like—are primarily concerned with the inculcation of values. They have become, in fact, the chief value-givers of this age.

Try paying close attention to television commercials. What values do they espouse? Some appeal to fear (buy our travelers' checks because you're likely to be robbed on your next trip), some to logic, even to thrift (our car compares favorably to its chief competitors in the following ways, and is cheaper), some to snobbery (at an elegant country house, fashionably dressed people are drinking a certain brand of sparkling water), some to pure hedonism (on a miserable winter day in the city a young couple chances upon a travel agency; their eyes focus on a replica of a credit card on the window and they are instantly transported to a dreamy tropical paradise).

Keep watching, and an underlying pattern will emerge. About half of the commercials, whatever the subject matter, are based on a climactic moment: The cake has already been baked; the family and guests, their faces all aglow, are gathered around to watch an adorable three-year-old blow out the candles. The race is run and won; beautiful young people jump up and down in ecstasy as they reach for frosted cans of diet cola. Men are shown working at their jobs for all of a second and a half, then it's Miller time. Life at its best, these commercials teach, is an endless series of climactic moments.

And the sitcoms and soaps, the crime shows, and MTV all run on the same hyped-up schedule: (1) If you make smart-assed one-liners for a half hour, everything will work out fine in time for the closing commercials. (2) People are quite nasty, don't work hard, and get rich quickly. (3) No problem is so serious that it can't be resolved in the wink of an eye as soon as the gleaming barrel of a handgun appears. (4) The weirdest fantasy you can think of can be realized instantly and without effort.

In all of this, the specific content isn't nearly as destructive to mastery as is the *rhythm*. One epiphany follows another. One fantasy is crowded out by the next. Climax is piled upon climax. *There's no plateau.*

The Path of Endless Climax

Two generations of Americans have grown up in the television age, during which consumerism has achieved unprecedented dominance over our value system. It should come as no great surprise that many of us have the idea that our lives by all rights should consist of one climax after another. So what do we do when our own day-to-day existence doesn't match up? How do we keep those climactic moments coming without instruction or discipline or practice? It's easy. Take a drug.

Of course, it doesn't work. In the long run it destroys you. But who in the popular and commercial culture has much to say about the long run? Who would be willing to warn in their commercial messages that every attempt to achieve an endless series of climactic moments, whether drug-powered or not, ends like this?

The epidemic of gambling currently sweeping across the nation shows how explicit and blatant the campaign against any long-term effort has become. An ad for the Illinois lottery pictured a man scoffing at people buying savings bonds, and insisting that the only way an ordinary person could become a millionaire was by playing the lottery. The very first commercial seen during an ABC special on the crisis in our high schools showed a bull session among a group of attractive young people. The models for this commercial were probably over twenty-one, but could easily have passed for high schoolers. "I'm going for the Trans-Am," one of them said. Another informed her friends that she would take the Hawaiian vacation, and a third said he was going to win the cash prize of $50,000. While there seemed no doubt in these happy youths' minds that they were going to win the sweepstakes in question, they were statistically more likely to die by drowning in a cistern, cesspool, or well.

A radio commercial for another sweepstakes dramatized the story of a young man who was ashamed to be seen by his brother while cooking hamburgers in a fast food restaurant. He explains that he's working to buy tickets to a pro football game. The brother asks why he's doing that when he could try for the tickets in a sweepstakes. The young man is immediately convinced. He then burns the hamburger he's cooking and serves the french fries still frozen. "I don't care," he says happily. "I can win tickets. I don't need this job."

If you could impute some type of central intelligence to all of these commercial messages, you would have to conclude that the nation is bent on self-destruction. In any case, you might suspect that the disproportionate incidence of drug abuse in the United States, especially of drugs that give you a quick high, springs not so much from immoral or criminal impulses as from a perfectly understandable impulse to replicate the most visible, most compelling American vision of the good life—an endless series of climactic moments. This vision isn't just an invention of television. It resonates in the rhetoric about scoring ("I don't care how you win, just win"), about effortless learning, instant celebrities, instant millionaires, and the "number one" finger raised in the air when you score just once. It is the ruling entrepreneurial vision of America, even among young ghetto drug dealers. "Based on my experience," writes anthropologist Philippe Bourgois, who spent five years of living in and studying the culture of East Harlem, "I believe the assertion of the culture-of-poverty theorists that the poor have been badly socialized and do not share mainstream values is wrong. On the contrary, ambitious, energetic, inner-city youths are attracted to the underground economy precisely because they believe in the rags-to-riches American dream. Like many in the mainstream, they are frantically trying to get their piece of the pie as fast as possible."

The quick-fix, antimastery mentality touches almost everything in our lives. Look at modern medicine and pharmacology. "Fast, temporary relief" is the battle cry. Symptoms receive immediate attention; underlying causes remain in the shadows. More and more research studies show that most illnesses are caused by environmental factors or way of life. The typical twelve-minute office visit doesn't give the doctor time to get to know the patient's face, much less his or her way of life. It does give time for writing a prescription.

A pioneering study by Dr. Dean Ornish and his associates in San Francisco has proven conclusively that coronary artery disease, our number one cause of death, can be reversed by a long-term regimen of diet, moderate exercise, yoga, meditation, and group support. No drugs, no operations. This program has been criticized by some doctors as "too radical." If this is radical, then what do these doctors consider "conservative"? Is it a bypass operation that will split your chest wide open, that has a 5-percent chance of causing death, a 30-percent chance of causing neurological damage, a 50-percent chance of being unnecessary; an operation which might have to be repeated after a few years and which costs $30,000. But all that doesn't seem to matter. At least it's a quick fix.

Business and industry? Perhaps no other area of American life is more in need of the principles of mastery. "Gone is talk of balanced, long-term growth," writes Ralph E. Winter in a *Wall Street Journal* article on the current fad of streamlining. "Impatient shareholders and well-heeled corporate raiders have seen to that. Now anxious executives, fearing for their jobs or their companies, are focusing their efforts on trimming operations and shuffling assets to improve near-term profits, often at the expense of both balance and growth." The leveraged buyout sums it all up. There's an enormous climax. Certain people make a lot of money in a short time. Very little if any real value is added to the corporation, or to the national economy. And the corporate raider becomes a culture hero.

But today's hero can become tomorrow's pariah. Already there are signs of a massive and growing disillusionment with our instant billionaires, and also with crash diets, miracle drugs both legal and illegal, lotteries, sweepstakes, and all the flash and clutter that accrues from the worship of quick, effortless success and fulfillment. If we need a reminder of just how disastrous the war against mastery can be, we have the S&L crisis, which brought quick rewards to a few and is bringing prolonged hardship to many. Make no mistake; it's all connected. The same climate of thought that would lead some people to the promise that they can learn a new skill or lose weight without patient, long-term effort leads others to the promise of great riches without the production of value in return.

A War That Can't Be Won

I'm aware that this critique of certain American values comes at a moment of great triumph for America and the West. Throughout the world, even in nations whose leaders revile us, there's a rising desire for the American way of life. Totalitarian governments are standing on very shaky ground these days. The hunger for free democratic governance has never been

...onger. Communism, with its centralized economic planning and control, is in full retreat. Freedom is doubtless the way to go. And throughout most of the world it's growing clear that nations need the system of feedback and individual incentive that obtains in a free market economy.

The victory is real and celebration is in order. But so is some cautious self-examination, for there's perhaps no more dangerous time for any society than its moment of greatest triumph. It would be truly foolish to let the decline of communism blind us to the long-term contradictions in a free market economy unrestrained by considerations of the environment and social justice, and driven by heedless consumerism, instant gratification, and the quick fix. Our dedication to growth at all costs puts us on a collision course with the environment. Our dedication to the illusion of endless climaxes puts us on a collision course with the human psyche.

Mastery applies to nations as well as to individuals. Our present national prosperity is built on a huge deficit and trillions of dollars worth of overdue expenditures on environmental cleanup, infrastructure repair, education, and social services—the quick-fix mentality. The failure to deal with the deficit goes along with easy credit and the continuing encouragement of individual consumption at the expense of saving and longer term gain. The celebration of results over process is reflected in shoddy workmanship and the ascendency of imported products. The urgent commercial appeals that paint life as a series of climactic moments are not unrelated to the current epidemics of drug abuse and gambling. Full shelves in the supermarkets and full lanes on the superhighways don't make up for the pitiful cries of crack babies, the breakdown of learning in and out of the schools, and the growing disparity between the rich and the poor.

America is still the most exciting of nations. Its freedom, its energy, its talent for innovation still inspire the world. But our time of grace might be running out. In the long run, the war against mastery, the path of patient, dedicated effort without attachment to immediate results, is a war that can't be won.

Chapter 4

Loving the Plateau

Early in life, we are urged to study hard, so that we'll get good grades. We are told to get good grades so that we'll graduate from high school and get into college. We are told to graduate from high school and get into college so that we'll get a good job. We are told to get a good job so that we can buy a house and a car. Again and again we are told to do one thing only so that we can get something else. We spend our lives stretched on an iron rack of contingencies.

Contingencies, no question about it, are important. The achievement of goals is important. But the real juice of life, whether it be sweet or bitter, is to be found not nearly so much in the products of our efforts as in the process of living itself, in how it feels to be alive. We are taught in countless ways to value the product, the prize, the climactic moment. But even after we've just caught the winning pass in the

Superbowl, there's always tomorrow and tomorrow and tomorrow. If our life is a good one, a life of mastery, most of it will be spent on the plateau. If not, a large part of it may well be spent in restless, distracted, ultimately self-destructive attempts to escape the plateau. The question remains: Where in our upbringing, our schooling, our career are we explicitly taught to value, to enjoy, even to love the plateau, the long stretch of diligent effort with no seeming progress?

I was fortunate in my middle years to have found aikido, a discipline so difficult and resistant to the quick fix that it showed me the plateau in sharp, bold relief. When I first started, I simply assumed that I would steadily improve. My first plateaus were relatively short and I could ignore them. After about a year and a half, however, I was forced to recognize that I was on a plateau of formidable proportions. This recognition brought a certain shock and disappointment, but somehow I persevered and finally experienced an apparent spurt of learning. The next time my outward progress stopped, I said to myself, "Oh damn. Another plateau." After a few more months there was another spurt of progress, and then, of course, the inevitable plateau. This time, something marvelous happened. I found myself thinking, "Oh boy. Another plateau. Good. I can just stay on it and keep practicing. Sooner or later, there'll be another spurt." It was one of the warmest moments on my journey.

The Joy of Regular Practice

At that time, the aikido school I attended was only eighteen months old, and there were no regular students above blue belt. Our teachers, the only black belts around, seemed to exist in an entirely different plane from the one on which we moved. I never even considered the possibility that I would rise to that rarefied plane. So there I was—an impatient, rather driven person who had always gone for the quickest, most direct route to a given goal—practicing regularly and hard for no particular goal at all, just for its own sake. Months would pass with no break in the steady rhythm of my practice. It was something new in my life, a revelation. The endless succession of classes was rewarding precisely because it was, in the Zen sense, "nothing special."

I went to class three or four times a week, from seven to nine P.M. When it was time to drive to the dojo (practice hall) in the city, the problems and distractions of the day began falling away. Just folding the quilted white cotton gi practice uniform softened my breathing and brought me a feeling of peace. The drive took about a half hour, across the bridge into the city, over a long hill that taxed my car's lowest gear, then finally down to a broad and noisy avenue noted for row upon row of car dealerships. Despite the noise outside, climbing the stairs to the second-story dojo was like entering a sanctuary, a place both alien to my customary existence and altogether familiar.

I loved everything about it, the ritual that was always the same yet always new: bowing upon entering, pulling my membership card from the rack on the front desk, changing to my gi in the dressing room. I loved the comforting smell of sweat, the subdued talk. I loved coming out of the dressing room and checking to see which other students were already warming up. I loved bowing again as I stepped on the mat, feeling the cool firm surface on the soles of my feet. I loved taking my place in the long row of aikidoists all sitting in seiza, the Japanese meditation position. I loved the entry of our teacher, the ritual bows, the warm-up techniques, and then my heart pounding, my breath rushing as the training increased in speed and power.

It wasn't always like that. Sometimes, when the moment came to go to class, I would be feeling particularly lazy. On those occasions I would be tempted to do almost anything rather than face myself once again on the mat. And sometimes I would give in to that inevitable human resistance against doing what's best for us, and waste an evening distracting myself.

I knew quite well, however, that when I did overcome my lethargy, I would be rewarded with a little miracle: I knew that, no matter how I felt on climbing the dojo stairs, two hours later—after hundreds of throws and falls—I would walk out tingling and fully alive, feeling so good, in fact, that the night itself would seem to sparkle and gleam.

This joy, I repeat, had little to do with progress or the achievement of goals. I was taken totally by surprise, in fact, when one of my teachers called a fellow student and me into his office after a weekend of marathon training and handed us brown belts, the rank next to black belt. One night about a year later, the four most advanced brown belts in the school happened to have a conversation during which we obliquely touched upon the possibility that we ourselves might someday achieve the rank of black belt. The idea was both exciting and troubling, and when I next came to class I was aware of something new: the worm of ambition was eating stealthily away at the center of my belly.

Maybe it was coincidence, but within three weeks of that conversation all four of us suffered serious injuries—a broken toe, torn ligaments in the elbow, a dislocated shoulder (mine), and an arm broken in three places. These injuries were effective teachers. After recovering, we settled back into steady, goalless practice. Another year and a half was to pass before the four of us made black belt.

This isn't to say that we didn't practice hard. The Hacker gets on a plateau and doesn't keep working. As I think back on that period, I realize that in spite of our many flaws we were definitely on the path of mastery. Unlike the Hacker, we were working hard, doing the best we could to improve our skills. But we had learned the perils of getting ahead of ourselves, and now were willing to stay on the plateau for as long as was necessary. Ambition still was there, but it was tamed. Once again we enjoyed our training. We loved the plateau. *And* we made progress.

This essential paradox becomes especially clear in a martial art that is exceptionally demanding, unforgiving, and rewarding. But it holds true, I think, in every human activity that involves significant learning—mental, physical, emotional, or spiritual. And despite our society's urgent and effective war against mastery, there are still millions of people who, while achieving great things in their work, are dedicated to the process as well as to the product—people who love the plateau. Life for these people is especially vivid and satisfying.

"It's my truest happiness," a writer friend told me. "It's the time when all the crap goes away. As soon as I walk into my study, I start getting cues of pleasure—my books on the shelves, the particular odor of the room. These cues begin to tie into what I've written and what I'm going to write. Even if I've stayed up all night, my fatigue disappears, just like that. There's a whole range of pleasure waiting for me, from making one sentence work to getting a new insight.''

''A lot of people go for things only because a teacher told them they should, or their parents,'' said Olympic gymnast Peter Vidmar. ''People who get into something for the money, the fame, or the medal can't be effective. When you discover you own desire, you're not going to wait for other people to find solutions to your problems. You're going to find your own. I set goals for myself, but underlying all the goals and the work was the fact that I enjoyed it. I thought gymnastics was fun. And I had no idea that I might someday be an Olympian.''

''The routine is important to me,'' said a successful painter who works in her studio for four hours five times a week. ''When I get started, there's a wonderful sense of well-being. I like to feel myself plodding along. I specifically choose that word, *plod*. When it's going good, I feel 'this is the essential me.' It's the routine itself that feeds me. If I didn't do it, I'd be betraying the essential me.''

When I was a boy, my father would let me go to his office with him on Saturday mornings. I don't think he had to go. He was simply drawn there; it was his place of practice. He was in the fire insurance business, and while he went through his mail, he would let me wander through the office, free to play with the marvelous mechanical contrivances of those days—the stately upright typewriters, the hand-operated adding machines, the staplers and paper punches, and the old dictaphone on which I could record a thin facsimile of my voice.

I loved the Saturday morning silence and the smells of glue and ink, rubber erasers and well-worn wood. I would play with the machines and make paper air-planes for a while but then, more likely than not, I would go into my father's office and just sit there watching him, fascinated by the depth of his concentration. He was in a world of his own, entirely relaxed and at the same time entirely focused as he opened the envelopes of various sizes and shapes, sorted the contents into piles, and made notes to his secretary. And all the time he worked, his lips were slightly parted, his breath steady and calm, his eyes soft, and his hands moving steadily, almost hypnotically. I remember wondering even then, when I was not more than ten years old, if I would ever have such a power of concentration or take such pleasure in my work. Certainly not at school, certainly not during my scattered, abortive attempts to do homework. I knew even then that he was an ambitious man with a burning desire for the extrinsic rewards of his work, including public recognition and even fame. But I also knew that he loved his work—the feel, the rhythm, the texture of it. My father's colleagues later told me that he was among the best in his field. Still, the public recognition he might have wished for never materialized, nor did the fame. But recognition is often unsatisfying and fame is like seawater for the thirsty. Love of your work, willingness to stay with it even in the absence of extrinsic reward, is good food and good drink.

The Face of Mastery

The look of deep concentration on my father's face as he did the work he loved is not unlike the expression that can be seen on the face of almost anyone on the path of mastery—even in the throes of physical exertion. Sports photography as we know it has been captured by the "thrill of victory/agony of defeat" school. Again and again we're shown climactic moments (prodigious exertion, faces contorted with pain or triumph), almost to the exclusion of anything else. But it seems to me that mastery's true face is relaxed and serene, sometimes faintly smiling. In fact, those we most admire in sports seem at times to enter another dimension. Besieged by opposing players, battered by the screams of the crowd, they make fficult, even the supernatural, seem easy, and manage somehow to create harmony where chaos might otherwise prevail.

In preparing the *Esquire* special on mastery, I decided to see if I could find a series of pictures that would illustrate The Face of Mastery. I went through hundreds of prints and transparencies from the major photo agencies, and there, scattered among the "thrill of victory/agony of defeat" shots, was just what I was looking for: Steven Scott making the last turn in a mile race, his face serene, his body relaxed; Greg Louganis at the edge of the diving board, his face a study in calm concentration; Peter Vidmar doing floor exercises, his body in an impossibly strenuous position, his face reflective and composed; Kareem Abdul-Jabbar launching his "sky-hook" basketball shot over the hand of an opposing player, his face a revelation of inner delight. Abdul-Jabbar is not a man of small ego. I'm sure he loved the money, the fame, the privileges his career brought him. But he loved the sky-hook more.

Goals and contingencies, as I've said, are important. But they exist in the future and the past, beyond the pale of the sensory realm. Practice, the path of mastery, exists only in the present. You can see it, hear it, smell it, feel it. To love the plateau is to love the eternal now, to enjoy the inevitable spurts of progress and the fruits of accomplishment, then serenely to accept the new plateau that waits just beyond them. To love the plateau is to love what is most essential and enduring in your life.

 PART TWO

THE FIVE
MASTER KEYS

Introduction

The human individual is equipped to learn and go on learning prodigiously from birth to death, and this is precisely what sets him or her apart from all other known forms of life. Man has at various times been defined as a building animal, a working animal, and a fighting animal, but all of these definitions are incomplete and finally false. Man is a learning animal, and the essence of the species is encoded in that simple term.

In this light, the mastery of skills that are not genetically programmed is the most characteristically human of all activities. The first and best of this learning involves no formal arrangements whatever; the world itself is school enough. We all participate in a master's journey in early childhood when we learn to talk or to walk. Every adult or older child around us is a teacher of language—the type of teacher who smiles at success, permits approximations, and isn't likely to indulge in lectures (i.e., the best type). We achieve an upright stance and bipedal locomotion with the help of the same encouraging, permissive instructors, along with the immediate and decisive assistance of gravity—a master teacher if ever there was one. Then, too, humans are genetically predisposed toward language and bipedal locomotion.

Later, however, we face the task of learning skills for which there's no cooperative surrounding environment, skills for which we aren't as genetically predisposed to develop. (Neither jet planes nor grand pianos were involved in the early evolution of homo sapiens.) More and more as we emerge into the teen and adult years, we must find our own doors to mastery. Chapters Five through Nine present five keys to opening those doors.

Chapter 5

Key 1: Instruction

There are some skills you can learn on your own, and some you can try to learn, but if you intend to take the journey of mastery, the best thing you can do is to arrange for first-rate instruction. The self-taught person is on a chancy path. There are advantages: you enjoy the license of not knowing what *can't* be done; you might wander into fertile territory previously ruled out by mainline explorers. Some of those who have taught themselves—Edison for one, Buckminster Fuller for another—have made it work. Most, however, have spent their lives reinventing the wheel, then refusing to concede that it's out of round. Even those who will some day overthrow conventional ways of thinking or doing need to know what it is they are overthrowing.

Instruction comes in many forms. For mastering most skills, there's nothing better than being in the hands of a master teacher, either one-to-one or in a small group. But there are also books, films, tapes, computer learning programs, computerized simulators (flight simulators, for example), group instruction, the classroom, knowledgeable friends, counselors, business associates, even "the street." Still, the individual teacher or coach can serve as a standard for all forms of instruction, the first and brightest beacon on the journey of mastery.

The search for good instruction starts with a look at credentials and lineage. Who was your teacher's teacher? Who was that teacher's teacher? And so on back to the timeless time when individual identity disappears in the myth of first beginnings. These are perhaps quaint questions in an age that has let the cord of lineage come almost completely unravelled, but good questions nonetheless. (Even tapes and books and computer learning programs have an ancestry.)

Respect for credentials, however, shouldn't blind you to other considerations. The instructor who advertises as an eighth-degree black belt in one martial art, ninth-degree in another, and light-middleweight champion of the world in both could be a lousy teacher. John McEnroe might turn up in later years as a superb tennis coach—but he might not. The teaching tactics of a Nobel laureate could turn out to be poison for the mind of a neophyte physicist. It's particularly challenging, in fact, for a top performer to become a first-rate teacher. Instruction demands a certain humility; at best, the teacher takes delight in being surpassed by his or her students. Gymnastics coach Bela Karole would have a very hard time performing the moves he has taught to both Nadia Comaneci of Romania and Mary Lou Retton of the USA.

To see the teacher clearly, look at the students. They are his work of art. If at all possible, attend an instructional session before choosing your teacher. Focus your attention on the students. Even more, on the *interaction*. Does the instructor proceed through praise or through damnation? There is the brand of teacher, often celebrated in myth if not in reality, who is famous for giving an absolute minimum of praise. When this teaching tactic works, it's through an economic principle, praise becoming so scarce a commodity that even a curt nod of grudging approval is taken to be highly rewarding. What doesn't work, despite a certain macho attitude to the contrary, is scorn, excoriation, humiliation—anything that destroys the student's confidence and self-esteem. Even the praise-stingy teacher must in some way show respect for the student in order to get long-term positive results. The best teacher generally strives to point out what the student is doing right at least as frequently as what she or he is doing wrong, which is just what UCLA coach John Wooden, perhaps the greatest basketball mentor of all time, managed to do all through his long, winning career. Wooden was observed to maintain approximately a fifty-fifty ratio between reinforcement and correction, with exceptional enthusiasm on both sides of the equation.

Look again at the students, the interaction. Do the more talented, more advanced students get all the goodies? How about the klutzes, the beginners? Maybe you're looking for the type of instructor who's comfortable only with the best, only with potential champions. There are such teachers, and they serve a useful function, but for me the essence of the instructor's art lies in the ability to work effectively and enthusiastically with beginners and to serve as a guide on the path of mastery for those who are neither as fast nor as talented as the norm. This service can be listed under altruism, but it's more than that. For to participate with a beginner in the first faltering mental and physical moves involved in learning a new skill is to penetrate the inner structure not only of that skill but also of the process of mastery itself. Knowledge, expertise, technical skill, and credentials are important, but without the patience and empathy that go with teaching beginners, these merits are as nothing.

The Best of Instructors, the Worst of Instructors

It was at the high-water mark of a war that had surged all the way around the globe that I first found myself in the instructor's role. The top six graduates of Class 44-C of the advanced flight school at Turner Field in Albany, Georgia—brand new second lieutenants with silver pilot's wings—were kept back and made flight instructors while the other 304 graduates were sent on to combat. Far from being pleased with our assignments, the six of us professed a burning desire for immediate combat duty, a sentiment that became maudlin after a few drinks at the officers club on our nights off. I was twenty years old. The other five new instructors were about the same age.

In March of 1944, despite our lack of experience, we were assigned students, and, without a word of advice, sent up to teach them to fly the B-25, a high-performance medium bomber of the time. The invasion of Fortress Europe was imminent. The Pacific campaign, it was predicted, would last for years. Pilots, like the planes they would fly, had to be produced by the tens of thousands, never mind such niceties as stringent safety procedures.

Flying conditions would have caused a major scandal in peacetime. Even on the darkest nights, with giant thunderstorms closing in, some hundred B-25s would jockey for position in the landing pattern at the end of each instructional period. There was nothing like a radar traffic control system; our lives hung on visual acuity, flying skill, and fast reflexes. During the summer of 1944, two spectacular midair collisions at Turner Field resulted in the destruction of four planes and the tragic loss of the instructors and cadets flying them. The crashes never made the newspapers. There was no time for sympathy or second chances. Student pilots who didn't measure up were washed out, discarded like defective components coming off a production line.

The six months I spent at Turner Field proved to be more challenging, and actually more dangerous, than the combat tour in the South Pacific that followed. After logging 600 hours as a flight instructor under the most demanding of conditions, I had gained a sure sense of the mastery of flight that has never left me.

And what about my students? Ah, that's another story.

Time provides no replays. But I am left, after all of these years, with crystalline memories of preternaturally white clouds soaring over deep green fields of cotton and corn, of the insistent engine sound that finally became no sound at all, of smoking engines and failed hydraulic systems, of illegal flights out over the Atlantic to play vertiginous games of follow-the-leader with other planes while our students held their breaths. But more than anything, I am left with a morality tale on the subject of instructing, in which I play the leading role. There's nothing I can do to change it. I was the best of instructors. I was the worst of instructors. The first does not justify the second.

Each of us was given four students to guide through the entire two months of advanced training. I quickly discovered that two of my students—cadets by the name of Stull and Thatcher—were quite talented. The other two—call them Brewster and Edmundson—were, at best, mediocre. This discrepancy suggested a plan: I would keep Stull and Thatcher together. I'd never let them fly with anyone else; they would be safe from contamination by lesser talents. This would allow me to initiate the two of them into a mode of flying a fellow instructor and I had developed while still cadets. We called it maximum performance, and it simply meant that we would fly as close as possible to perfection at all times, even when regulations didn't call for it, even when no one was watching.

And so, without mentioning the words maximum performance, I set standards for Stull and Thatcher approximately ten times more stringent than what was called for. Normally, while flying on instruments, pilots were given a leeway of 200 feet above or below the prescribed altitude, but I led Stull and

Thatcher to believe they had only a 20-foot margin of error. I insisted they hold their gyro compass heading right on the money at all times. I taught them, even when landing on a 10,000-foot runway, to touch down on the first hundred feet.

I gave Stull and Thatcher my very best, and they responded just as I had hoped they would. Even though I never let them fly with other cadets, they must have compared notes and figured out what I was up to. Sometimes, when I described a particularly unreasonable standard of performance with a straight face, they were unable to keep from smiling. After the first few weeks, I too couldn't keep a smile off my face. We were joined in a delicious conspiracy of excellence. On the days I was scheduled to fly with them, I awakened with a feeling of excitement and anticipation.

I can still see Stull and Thatcher with incredible clarity, one of them in the pilot's seat, the other standing in back and leaning down between the pilot's and copilot's seats to watch yet another perfect approach and landing. The pure, prophetic light of another time still pours in through the Plexiglas canopy—the towering clouds, the impossible blue of the sky—and the two cadets' faces still glow with the incomparable happiness that comes when you first embark on the journey of mastery.

Now for the hard part of the story.

After my first few flights with the cadets I'm calling Brewster and Edmundson, I simply lost interest. I was too young, too impatient, too arrogant in my espousal of maximum performance to endure their rather inept efforts at flying the B-25. Brewster was slim, patrician, and shy. Edmundson was heavy-set and confident, the squadron jokester. On one flight I thought he made a snide remark at my expense. I took the controls, climbed to 10,000 feet, and racked the plane around in maneuvers it was never meant to perform, leaving Edmundson and Brewster pale and shaken.

I went through the motions. Now and then I made an effort to bring them along, to discover what was blocking their progress, to develop their potential to its fullest extent. But my enthusiasms were short-lived. Some particularly blatant display of crudity on the controls by Edmundson or tentativeness on the part of Brewster would cause me to shake my head in despair and disgust, and either turn away and slump in my seat or take the controls and show them exactly how the maneuver should be done.

As it turned out, Brewster and Edmundson graduated along with Stull and Thatcher, but just barely. After the war, I happened to run into Brewster at a dance in Atlanta. He took the opportunity (the force of his resentment overcoming any shyness he might have felt) to let me know exactly what he thought about his experiences with me at Turner Field. I had no adequate reply. Long before that time, I had begun to feel guilty about the way I had handled my first assignment as an instructor. In fact, I never again segregated my students as I had done the first time. I graduated two more groups of pilots before leaving for combat, experiencing neither the exhilaration I had felt with Stull and Thatcher nor the despair I had felt with Brewster and Edmundson. I worked to control my impatience, to do the best I could with the slower students. Still, a continuing preoccupation with maximum performance, along with an extremity of youth, tended to frustrate my own performance as a teacher of the less talented.

The Magic of Teaching Beginners

Many years later, I found myself once again in the instructor's role, engaged this time in an art far more subtle and complex and difficult to learn than flying. I was forty-seven when a friend invited me to join the aikido class he was organizing. I had never heard of aikido, nor had I ever dreamed of becoming a martial artist. That was twenty years ago, and I can now say that practicing aikido has been the second most profound learning experience of my life. Teaching aikido has been the most profound.

Even before getting my first-degree black belt, I

was enlisted by my teacher as an assistant instructor. My job: teaching the basics of the art to beginners. Six years later, in October 1976, shortly after getting our black belts, two of my fellow aikidoists and I started our own dojo. From rather questionable beginnings fourteen years ago (it's not customary for first-degree black belts to start their own school), Aikido of Tamalpais has become a respected and happy dojo. We three founders have continued developing our skills, and have advanced to higher ranks. From the thousands of students who have practiced at our school for varying lengths of time have come twenty-eight black belts—not an insignificant number in a difficult art that offers no cheap degrees.

At this point, I'd like to be able to tell you that by now I've mastered the art of teaching slow students and beginners. But that wouldn't be true; I still have to work at it. I listen carefully when Wendy Palmer, one of my partners, tells me that teaching beginners and slow students is not only fascinating but pleasurable. The talented student, she believes, is likely to learn so fast that small stages in the learning process are glossed over, creating an opaque surface that hides the secrets of the art from view. With the slow student, though, the teacher is forced to deal with small, incremental steps that penetrate like X rays the very essence of the art, and clearly reveal the process which the art becomes manifest in move-

Gradually the mystery has unfolded. My experience as an instructor has shown me, for one thing, that the most talented students don't necessarily make the best martial artists. Sometimes, strangely enough, those with exceptional talent have trouble staying on the path of mastery. In 1987, my colleagues at *Esquire* and I conducted a series of interviews with athletes known as masters of their sports, which tended to confirm this paradoxical finding. Most of the athletes we interviewed stressed hard work and experience over raw talent. "I have seen so many baseball players with God-given ability who just didn't want to work," Rod Carew said. "They were soon gone. I've seen others with no ability to speak of who stayed in the big leagues for fourteen or fifteen years."

Good Horse, Bad Horse

In his book *Zen Mind, Beginner's Mind,* Zen master Shunryu Suzuki approaches the question of fast and slow learners in terms of horses. "In our scriptures, it is said that there are four kinds of horses: excellent ones, good ones, poor ones, and bad ones. The best horse will run slow and fast, right and left, at the driver's will, before it sees the shadow of the whip; the second best will run as well as the first one, just before the whip reaches its skin; the third one will run when it feels pain on its body; the fourth will run after the pain penetrates to the marrow of its bones. You can imagine how difficult it is for the fourth one to learn to run.

"When we hear this story, almost all of us want to be the best horse. If it is impossible to be the best one, we want to be the second best." But this is a mistake, Master Suzuki says. When you learn too easily, you're tempted not to work hard, not to penetrate to the marrow of a practice.

"If you study calligraphy, you will find that those who are not so clever usually become the best calligraphers. Those who are very clever with their hands often encounter great difficulty after they have reached a certain stage. This is also true in art, and in life." The best horse, according to Suzuki, may be the worst horse. And the worst horse can be the best, for if it perseveres, it will have learned whatever it is practicing all the way to the marrow of its bones.

Suzuki's parable of the four horses has haunted me ever since I first heard it. For one thing, it poses a clear challenge for the person with exceptional talent: to achieve his or her full potential, this person will have to work just as diligently as those with less innate ability. The parable has made me realize that if I'm the first or second horse as an instructor of fast learners, I'm the third or fourth horse as an instructor of slow learners. But there is hope. If I persevere and dedicate my efforts to bringing along every Brewster and Edmundson who shows up at our aikido school, I'll someday know this aspect of instructing all the way to the marrow of my bones.

So when you look for your instructor, in whatever skill or art, spend a moment celebrating it when you discover one who pursues maximum performance. But also make sure that he or she is paying exquisite attention to the slowest student on the mat.

Comparing Various Modes of Instruction

How about the other modes of instruction? In most cases, audio and video tapes have only limited effectiveness. Learning eventually involves interaction between the learner and the learning environment, and its effectiveness relates to the frequency, quality, variety, and intensity of the interaction. With tapes, there's no real interaction at all; information flows in one direction only. A videotape can show you an ideal golf swing to copy, and that's certainly better than nothing, but the tape has no way of observing your swing and telling you how well you're replicating the ideal. With remote control, the tape can be easily stopped, reversed, repeated, and in some cases played in slow motion—all of which makes it much better than instructional films or television programs, which march along at a steady rate, regardless of the learner's progress or understanding.

A book is also self-paced, and it's portable and handy. Like tape, its suffers from lack of feedback capability. Still, in spite of the marvels of the computer age, the book remains a major tool for learning especially in skills that are primarily cognitive. If a picture is sometimes worth a thousand words, then perhaps a moving picture is worth 10,000 words. But it's also true that one good paragraph sometimes has more power to change the individual and the world than any number of pictures.

The typical school or college classroom, unhappily, is not a very good place to learn. "Frontal teaching," with one instructor sitting or standing in front of twenty to thirty-five students who are sitting at fixed desks, is primarily an administrative expediency, a way of parceling out and keeping track of the flood of students in mass education. It's sad that over the past hundred years almost every aspect of our national life—industry, transportation, communication, computation, entertainment— has changed almost beyond recognition, while our schools remain essentially the same.

Take a look. There it is: one teacher giving out the same information at the same rate to a group of mostly passive students regardless of their individual abilities, cultural backgrounds, or learning styles. I've written at some length on this subject and on the type of reform that could remedy the situation through the self-pacing and individualizing capabilities of the computer and other new instructional modes. I believe that within ten or fifteen years at the most some sort of school reform along these lines is inevitable.

Meanwhile, there are still good teachers and bad teachers. Visits to hundreds of schools have convinced me that the teacher who can make the present system work is undoubtedly a master. He or she is not necessarily the one who gives the most polished lectures, but rather the one who has discovered *how to involve each student actively* in the process of learning. One award-winning mathematician at a major university was famous for intentionally making small mistakes when he wrote formulas on the chalkboard. Students sat on the edge of their chairs vying to be the first to catch the mistake and rush up to correct their professor—truly a master of the instructor's art.

Knowing When to Say Good-bye

Fortunate is the person who can find such a teacher, especially at the beginning of the learning process. Students at school up to and including college often don't have much choice. Even those of us who do have a choice sometimes make a bad one. If you should end up with a teacher who doesn't seem right for you, first look inside. You might well be expecting more than any teacher can give. But teachers as well as students can be lazy, excessively goal oriented, indifferent, psychologically seductive, or just plain inept. It's important to keep the proper psychological distance. If you're too far removed, there's no chance for the surrender that's part of the master's journey (see Chapter Seven); if you come too close, you lose all perspective and become a disciple rather than a student. The responsibility for good balance lies with student as well as teacher. When irreconcilable differences do occur, remember that the better part of wisdom is knowing when to say good-bye.

Bear in mind that on the path of mastery learning never ends. In the words of the great Japanese swordmaster Yamaoka Tesshu:

> *Do not think that*
> *This is all there is.*
> *More and more*
> *Wonderful teachings exist—*
> *The sword is unfathomable.*

Chapter 6

Key 2: Practice

It's an old joke that appears in many versions but always sends the same message. In one version, a couple of Texans in a Cadillac on their way to a concert are lost in New York's Lower East Side. They stop to question a bearded elder.

"How do you get to Carnegie Hall?" they ask.

"Practice!" he tells them.

That usage of the word—practice as a verb—is clear to all of us. You practice your trumpet, your dance routine, your multiplication tables, your combat mission. To practice in this sense implies something separate from the rest of your life. You practice in order to learn a skill, in order to improve yourself, in order to get ahead, achieve goals, make money. This way of thinking about practice is useful in our society; you obviously have to practice to get to Carnegie Hall.

MASTERY

For one who is on the master's journey, however, the word is best conceived of as a noun, not as something you *do,* but as something you *have,* something you *are.* In this sense, the word is akin to the Chinese word tao and the Japanese word do, both of which mean, literally, road or path. Practice is the path upon which you travel, just that.

A practice (as a noun) can be anything you practice on a regular basis as an integral part of your life—not in order to gain something else, but for its own sake. It might be a sport or a martial art. It might be gardening or bridge or yoga or meditation or community service. A doctor practices medicine and an attorney practices law, and each of them also *has* a practice. But if that practice is only a collection of patients or clients, a way of making a living, it isn't a *master's* practice. For a master, the rewards gained along the way are fine, but they are not the main reason for the journey. Ultimately, the master and the master's path are one. And if the traveler is fortunate—that is, if the path is complex and profound enough—the destination is two miles farther away for every mile he or she travels.

A woman in one of our workshops asked my wife, Annie, why she was still going to aikido classes. "I thought you'd already gotten your black belt," she said. It took Annie a few minutes to explain that a black belt is only one more step along an endless path, a license to go on learning for as long as you live.

In a nation obsessed with the achievement of goals ("It doesn't matter how you score; the score is all that counts." "Don't tell me how you are going to sell the ad, just sell it." "Winning isn't everything; it's the only thing."), devotion to the goalless journey might seem incomprehensible if not bizarre. But behind the slogans you read on the sports page and in the business section there's a deeper reality: the master goes along with the rhetoric about scoring and winning (in today's media climate, who would listen to anything else?), but secretly cherishes those games filled with delicious twists and turns of fortune, great plays, close calls, and magical finishes—regardless of who wins.

There's another secret: The people we know as masters don't devote themselves to their particular skill just to get better at it. The truth is, *they love to practice*—and because of this they do get better. And then, to complete the circle, the better they get the more they enjoy performing the basic moves over and over again.

Beginners at the basics classes at our aikido school will do a simple blending move about eight or ten times, then start looking around restlessly for something new to distract them. Black belts at the basics classes have the knowledge and experience—the

feel—necessary to appreciate the subtleties and endless possibilities contained within even the most ru-
dimentary technique. I remember an aikido class
years ago when I was a brown belt, the rank just
below black belt. Our teacher started us doing a technique called shiho-nage (four-way throw), then continued with the same variation of the same technique
for the entire two-hour class. After the first half hour,
I began wondering what was coming next. (Our
school rarely practiced the same technique for so
long a time.) By the end of the first hour, however,
I had settled into a steady, trancelike rhythm that
obliterated all considerations of time or repetition.
My perceptions expanded. The barely noticeable
variations from one throw to the next became significant and revealing. By the end of the second hour,
I was hoping that the class would go on until mid-
night, that it would never end.

Staying on the Mat

"The master," an old martial arts saying goes, "is
the one who stays on the mat five minutes longer
every day than anybody else." And not just in aikido.
In August 1988, I visited the Seattle Seahawks' training camp as a guest of the team's offensive coordi-
nator. When the morning practice session was over,
the players shambled off the field to the dressing

room—all of the players except two, that is. One of the two kept running out, then wheeling suddenly to take a pass from the other. Again and again, he ran the same pattern, caught the same pass. The field was empty; the other players were inside taking their showers, getting dressed. The coaches, too, were gone and the spectators had drifted away. I remained there on the sidelines, fascinated. Who was this eager pass receiver? Surely, it was some brand new rookie, someone trying to get good enough to make the team. No, it was Steve Largent, not only the premier pass receiver of the Seattle Seahawks but the leading receiver in the history of the National Football League.

The master of any game is generally a master of practice. In his prime, Larry Bird of the Boston Celtics was perhaps the most complete basketball player of all time. Unable to jump as high or run as fast as many other players, he was named National Basketball Association Rookie of the Year for 1980, Most Valuable Player in two championship series, and the league MVP for three years in a row. Bird began developing his basketball practice at age four, and never stopped practicing. After the Celtics won the NBA championship in June 1986, reporters asked Bird what he planned to do next. "I've still got some things I want to work on," he was quoted as saying. "I'll start my off-season training next week. Two hours a day, with at least a hundred free throws.'' Many professionals take some of the summer off, but not Larry Bird. He runs for conditioning, up and down the steepest hills he can find. On the blacktop court with glass backboard at home in French Lick, Indiana, he practices. During the season, in the Hellenic College gym in Brookline, he practices. On road trips, in arenas all around the country, before every game, he practices.

During his years with the Celtics, Bird was known for getting on the court an hour or two before everyone else to practice his shots—foul shots, fall-away shots, three-pointers, shots from all sorts of angles. Sometimes, just for fun, he would sit on the sideline and pop them in, or find a seat in the first row and float them in. No question, Bird likes to win. Still, according to his agent Bob Woolf, that's not the main reason he practices so diligently and plays so wholeheartedly. ''He does it just to enjoy himself. Not to make money, to get acclaim, to gain stature. He just loves to play basketball.''

Explicit skills such as those found in martial arts, sports, dance, music, and the like provide explicit examples of practice. But this second key to mastery undergirds a wide variety of human endeavors. Good business practice demands that managers keep the mechanics of their operations current at all times, being especially diligent and disciplined in such basic matters as budget, order fulfillment, and quality control. Families that stay together hold fast to certain rituals regardless of the haste and distractions of daily life; this might mean having one full, sit-down meal every day with every family member present. Nations also have their practice, as seen, for example, in the regular and heartfelt observance of national festivals and sacred days. This nation indulges in a questionable experiment in casually changing the dates of its holidays ("holy days") for the sake of commerce and four-day weekends.

To practice regularly, even when you seem to be getting nowhere, might at first seem onerous. But the day eventually comes when practicing becomes a treasured part of your life. You settle into it as if into your favorite easy chair, unaware of time and the turbulence of the world. It will still be there for you tomorrow. It will never go away.

"How long will it take me to master aikido?" a prospective student asks. "How long do you expect to live?" is the only respectable response. Ultimately, practice *is* the path of mastery. If you stay on it long enough, you'll find it to be a vivid place, with its ups and downs, its challenges and comforts, its surprises, disappointments, and unconditional joys. You'll take your share of bumps and bruises while traveling—bruises of the ego as well as of the body, mind, and spirit—but it might well turn out to be the most reliable thing in your life. Then, too, it might eventually make you a winner in your chosen field, if that's what you're looking for, and then people will refer to you as a master.

But that's not really the point. What is mastery? At the heart of it, mastery is practice. Mastery is staying on the path.

Chapter 7

Key 3: Surrender

The courage of a master is measured by his or her willingness to surrender. This means surrendering to your teacher and to the demands of your discipline. It also means surrendering your own hard-won proficiency from time to time in order to reach a higher or different level of proficiency.

The early stages of any significant new learning invoke the spirit of the fool (see the Epilogue). It's almost inevitable that you'll feel clumsy, that you'll take literal or figurative pratfalls. There's no way around it. The beginner who stands on his or her dignity becomes rigid, armored; the learning can't get through. This doesn't mean that you should surrender your own physical and moral center or passively accept teachings that would be bad for you. But you've already checked out your instructor (see Key 1). Now's the time for a certain suspension of disbelief. So your teacher asks you to begin by putting your finger on your nose and standing on one foot. Unless there's some compelling reason to the contrary, just surrender. Give it a try.

After all, learning almost any significant skill involves certain indignities. Your first few dives are likely to be belly flops—and they'll draw the attention of almost everyone at the pool. Are you willing to accept that? If not, forget diving. The face you draw in your first art class looks more like Mr. Potato Head than the Mona Lisa. Is that a good reason for giving up art? And how about those fluttering ankles the first few times you try ice skating? And the impact of the hard, cold ice on the part of the body normally reserved for spankings? Punishment of this sort isn't limited to beginners; it happens in the Olympics. If you want to get there, be prepared to take it.

And then there are the endless repetitions, the drudgery, the basic moves practiced over and over again. Who but a fool would embark on a musical career in the full knowledge that he or she might end up repeating all the major and minor scales perhaps a hundred thousand times each? To some people that prospect alone might seem to justify resisting any surrender. About halfway through my third aikido class, my teacher demonstrated tai no henko, the most basic blending movement in the art. Without a moment's thought, I heard myself saying, "We've already done that technique." That remark didn't even elicit a reply, just a faintly amused smile. My surrender was definitive: since then, I've practiced tai no henko at least 50,000 times.

Actually, the essence of boredom is to be found in the obsessive search for novelty. Satisfaction lies in mindful repetition, the discovery of endless richness in subtle variations on familiar themes.

Swordmaster Stories

The literature of the East is loaded with swordmaster-and-apprentice stories. All have the same general drift. A young man learns of a master of the sword who lives in a far province. After a long and difficult journey, he presents himself at the master's door and asks to become his student. The master closes the door in the young man's face. Every day thereafter, the young man comes to sit on the master's doorstep, simply waiting. A year passes, and the master grudgingly allows the young man to do chores around the house—chop wood, carry water. Months more go by, maybe years. One morning, without warning, the master attacks the young man from behind and whacks him on the shoulder with a bamboo sword, a shinai. The master has begun to teach alertness. At length, the master gives his apprentice his own shinai and continues teaching him the art of the sword, to which the student has been surrendering all along.

In a nation that has made a book entitled *Total Fitness in 12 Minutes a Week* into a national bestseller, such stories might tend to have little meaning. Still, the swordmaster myth has the power to penetrate our popular culture, if only in an Americanized version. The first, and best, *Karate Kid* movie condenses the years of the myth into a few months, having the apprentice painting the karate master's fence and waxing his car rather than chopping wood and carrying water.

Surrendering to your teacher and to the fundamentals of the art are only the beginning. There are times in almost every master's journey when it becomes necessary to give up some hard-won competence in order to advance to the next stage. This is especially true when you're stuck at a familiar and comfortable skill level. The parable of the cup and the quart applies here. There's a quart of milk on the table— within your reach. But you're holding a cup of milk in your hand and you're afraid to let go of the cup in order to get the quart.

Your fear isn't without foundation. If you've been shooting in the nineties for quite a while on the golf links and want to get your score down into the eighties or even the seventies, you might well have to give up the nineties for a while; you might have to take your game apart before putting it back together. This is true of almost any skill. For many years I had played jazz piano for my own amusement. I had developed a small repertory in a limited set of keys using rather unadventurous chording. Every time I wrote or spoke about the character I call the Hacker or looked at the curve describing the Hacker's progress, I thought about my own piano playing and said to myself, "That's me!"

About a year ago, egged on by my aikido partner, Wendy, a talented singer and guitarist, I found myself playing with a small jazz group, learning new songs in new keys, changing all of my chord voicing, and, in general, shooting for a level of play I had never dreamed of. At first everything started falling apart. Where was my comfortable old solo style? I had let go the cup and hadn't yet grasped the quart. I was floundering in the scary, slippery space between competencies.

Just then, we were given the opportunity of playing at a local jazz spot. Someone—could it have been me?—said, "Seize the day," and I found myself going straight from the land of the Hacker to the land of the Obsessive without even a side trip through the larger country of mastery, practicing so strenuously that I developed an inflamed tendon in my right little finger and had to ice my hand each time I played.

Somehow the performance passed without disaster, and now I'm groping my way toward the slow lane on the path of mastery in this skill.

A Tale of Two Experts

How do you respond when offered the chance of renouncing a present competency for a higher or different one? The story of two karate experts—call them Russell and Tony—trying to learn aikido might serve as a guide. Both of them were participants in an eight-week certification program that required aikido training five days a week. It was my job to teach the class.

Russell was small, wiry, intense, and scholarly—an exceptionally gracious person who went out of his way to be helpful to his fellow students. He held a doctorate, and was director of professional training in a large organization. In addition, he had a first-degree black belt in karate. Tony's schooling had been accomplished mostly on the streets of Jersey City. He had come to the martial arts early in life and now, at 31, he held a fourth-degree karate black belt and was owner of two karate schools.

From the moment Russell stepped on the training mat, he revealed that he was a trained martial artist. His individual warm-up routine included several karate moves. When called upon to deliver a punch during class, he resorted to the specialized style of his previous discipline. Once, on a two-hand grab attack, I noticed him moving purposefully to keep a maximum distance between his body and that of the person he was attacking. I suggested he stay closer and let himself flow with the attack. "Surely you jest," he said with a laugh. I told him that in order to learn the basic moves, it would be better just for now to forget defensive possibilities; we would learn to cover any openings later. I could see that Russell was finding it hard to let go of his expertise, and because of this failing to get the most out if his aikido training. After the first four weeks, he was falling behind some of those who had never done any martial art, and it was only at this point that he finally surrendered his prior competence and got on the path of mastery.

Tony's approach was different. From the beginning, he never made a move, not even a gesture, that might reveal he was an expert in another art. Without a hint of ostentation, he showed more respect than did any of the other students for his teachers—this in spite of his high rank. He carried himself with an air of calm sincerity and was unfailingly aware of everything going on around him. Along with this was a powerful presence that could be quickly recognized by any trained martial artist. Just by the way he sat, stood, and walked, Tony revealed himself as a fellow traveler on the path of mastery.

During a class at the end of the first four weeks, I had all the students sit at the edge of the mat, then asked Tony if he would show us one of his karate kata (predetermined sequence of movements). He bowed, walked to the center of the mat, and breathed deeply for a few moments. What followed brought a sharp intake of breath from almost all of us. Moving gracefully and faster than the eye could fully comprehend, Tony launched one swift and deadly strike and kick after another, leaping, spinning, emitting resounding kiai shouts as he dispatched imaginary foes at every point of the compass. When it was over, he once again bowed humbly and returned to the edge of the mat to take his place with the others—the most thoroughgoing beginner of them all.

Perhaps the best you can hope for on the master's journey—whether your art be management or marriage, badminton or ballet—is to cultivate the mind and heart of the beginning at every stage along the way. For the master, surrender means there are no experts. There are only learners.

Chapter 8

Key 4: Intentionality

It joins old words with new—character, willpower, attitude, imaging, the mental game—but what I'm calling intentionality, however you look at it, is an essential to take along on the master's journey.

The power of the mental game came to public awareness in the 1970s through the revelations of some of the nation's most notable sports figures. Golfer Jack Nicklaus, for example, let it be known that he never hit a shot without first clearly visualizing the ball's perfect flight and its triumphant destination, "sitting up there high and white and pretty on the green." A successful shot, Nicklaus told us, was 50 percent visualization, 40 percent setup, and only 10 percent swing. Premiere pro runningbacks described imaging each of their plays again and again the night before a game; they felt that their success on the field the next day was closely related to the vividness of their mental practice. Body builders and weightlifters testified to the value of intentionality. Arnold Schwarzenneger argued that pumping a weight one time with full consciousness was worth ten without mental awareness. He was joined by Frank Zane and others in vouching for the effect of the mind on such physical qualities as muscle and iron.

What had happened was that sports training and technique had reached an extremely high level of development—so high that further improvements along this line could come only in tiny increments. When Jack Nicklaus attributed only 10 percent of the success of a shot to the swing, it was perhaps because his swing was already nearly perfect. The realm of mind and spirit was the undiscovered land, the place where pioneers in sports performance could make the greatest gains.

To exploit this opportunity, a number of top-ranking teams and individuals have hired sports psychologists to teach relaxation, confidence, and the mental rehearsal of specific plays or moves. This has led to audiotapes and videotapes purported to hone the mental game for sports aspirants who can't afford their own psychologists. The messages on some of these tapes are less than sophisticated. Mind Communications, Inc., for example, puts out subliminal affirmations on audiotape. Beneath the sound of waves or "pink sound," certain words or phrases are spoken just below the level of ordinary awareness. The tape for football contains these phrases: "I know my plays. I am important. I can do it. I love to run. I relax. I use weights for strength. I get off the ball first. I avoid sugar, coffee, alcohol, tobacco. I love contact. I set a goal. I love exercise. I have good hands. I can beat my man. Drive, drive, drive. I breathe deeply and evenly. I am a winner." No research has yet been conducted to see if these messages make better football players.

Dr. Richard M. Suinn at Colorado State University has come up with a more sophisticated method called viseo-motor behavior rehearsal (VMBR), which combines exercises in deep relaxation with vivid mental imaging of the skill to be learned. In one study of VMBR, researchers at North Texas State University divided thirty-two students in a beginning karate class into four groups. They assigned each group a different practice to do at home during a six-week period in which they would meet twice a week for karate lessons. At the start, they gave each student baseline anxiety and skills tests, then launched them on their various types of practice: (1) deep muscle relaxation only; (2) imaging only—closing their eyes and doing karate moves in their mind's eye; (3) VMBR—relaxation exercises followed by imaging; and (4) no home practice. All the groups received traditional karate instruction.

At the end of the six weeks, the researchers again tested the students for anxiety, and the karate school gave its customary skill tests in basic moves and sparring. The VMBR and relaxation-only groups recorded lower levels of anxiety than the others. In sparring, the VMBR group clearly outscored the other three.

This test and others along the same line show results that are statistically significant but not spectacular. For one thing, the time period of most of these studies is relatively short; for another, the people used in the experiments are mostly beginners. These limitations make such studies less compelling than the numerous anecdotal reports of master athletes.

For me, the most compelling evidence of the power of imaging comes from direct experience on the aikido mat. Our particular lineage of the art employs many metaphors and images to go along with the mechanics of movement, and it is from the unsubstantial realm of mind or spirit that the most powerful physical results flow. For example, one version of nikkyo (a wrist lock) involves being grabbed at the wrist by an attacker, then holding the attacker's hand on your wrist while bringing your hand around and over his wrist and pressing downward at a certain angle. When performed properly, this subtle manuever can bring a much larger and stronger attacker to his or her knees.

A purely mechanical application of nikkyo might work, but only through the application of considerable muscular force. There are certain imaging strategies, however, that increase its effectiveness to a degree that isn't just "statistically significant," but truly startling. I ask my students to bring their hand, fingers extended, over the attacker's wrist as usual, then not to think of the wrist at all but rather "create" long extensions of these fingers to go right through the attacker's face like laser beams and touch the base of the skull. From this point, they simple stroke gently downward on the attacker's spine with their imaged finger extensions. All other things being equal, the effectiveness of the technique depends on the vividness of the image. In my own aikido practice, the imaged technique seems considerably more effective than muscular force alone; sometimes, an attacker goes down like a shot with a startled look on his face while I am unaware of using any muscular force at all.

What Is Really Real?

How do we explain the discrepancy between the mechanical and the imaged application? Are the magically extended fingers mere figments of the imagination or are they in some way "real"? The easiest explanation derives from mechanics alone: Perhaps the image of extended fingers stroking down the attacker's spine simply provides guidance for bringing the aikidoist into the proper alignment for the application of nikkyo. It certainly does that. But many years of experience have convinced me that more than alignment is involved. My logical mind tells me I don't really have fingers three feet long that can penetrate through another person's body to his or her spine. Still, the truly effortless, seemingly miraculous applications of the technique occur only when the mental image is vividly clear and when I can somehow "feel" my fingers moving down the attacker's spine.

Which brings us to the question of what is really "real." Is consciousness a mere epiphenomenon, as behaviorist B. F. Skinner would have it? Or is the poet William Blake right in suggesting that mental things alone are real? Or, if mental constructs and the stuff of the objective world are both real, though occupying different classes of reality, then what is the nature of the interaction between the two classes? These are large questions for a short book—even for a long one. Still, it's possible to say rather briefly (and obviously) that thought, images, feelings, and the like are quite real and that they do have a great influence on the world of matter and energy. Indeed, it's possible to argue that pure information is more persistent than what we class as substantial—or perhaps that both are at essence the same thing. "More and more, the universe looks like a great thought rather than a great machine," says astronomer Sir James Jeans.

Solomon's temple, for example, no longer exists in the form of wood, stone, and gold; you can't find it anywhere. Yet it bursts into graphic, detailed existence in your mind's eye when you read First Kings 6 and 7 of the Bible. Neither Scarlett O'Hara nor Anna Karenina were ever made flesh, yet it might be the case that you know them better than your next-door neighbor. Your portable transistor radio is certainly real; you can feel it in your hands. But so is the wiring diagram for that radio, and so is that diagram as it evolved in the mind of the inventor. Which is *more* real? It's hard to say. While the underlying structure, the abstract relationship among the parts, is the same in all three forms, it can be argued that what is most abstract is most fundamental and often most persistent over time. The diagram or the mental picture will probably outlast the radio you hold in your hands. And these insubstantial forms have an additional advantage: if you want to make changes in the relationships of the parts, it's easier to do so in the diagram or the mind than in the three-dimensional radio.

's the role of intentionality here? It's certainly involved in the creation of the structure-as-idea. It's also involved in the transformation of that structure from one of its forms to another. This sort of transformation, in fact, is what the process of mastery is all about. Sometimes I have my students hold the vision or the feeling of a certain throw in their mind, and then practice it over and over for an hour or more until they are drenched with sweat and wiped clean of their previous thoughts or feelings about the throw. This use of intentionality often produces favorable results in the palpable, three-dimensional world of the martial arts.

Thoughts, images, and feelings are indeed quite real. Einstein's thought that energy is equal to mass times the speed of light squared ($E = MC^2$) eventually unleashed awesome power. The transformation of that thought into heat and percussion was a long and arduous process. Still, the thought, the vision, the intentionality, was primary.

"All I know," said Arnold Schwarzenneger, "is that the first step is to create the vision, because when you see the vision there—the beautiful vision—that creates the 'want power.' For example, my wanting to be Mr. Universe came about because I saw myself so clearly, being up there on the stage and winning."

Intentionalty fuels the master's journey. Every master is a master of vision.

 **Chapter 9**

Key 5: The Edge

Now we come, as come we must in anything of real consequence, to a seeming contradiction, a paradox. Almost without exception, those we know as masters are dedicated to the fundamentals of their calling. They are zealots of practice, connoisseurs of the small, incremental step. At the same time—and here's the paradox—these people, these masters, are precisely the ones who are likely to challenge previous limits, to take risks for the sake of higher performance, and even to become obsessive at times in that pursuit. Clearly, for them the key is not either/or, it's both/and.

Chuck Yeager, the hero of Tom Wolfe's book *The Right Stuff,* is considered by many to be the best pilot who ever lived. Near the end of his autobiography, *Yeager,* he sums up what it means to be a great pilot, to have the "right stuff." In the first two pages of this summary, he cites "experience" three times. "If there is such a thing as the 'right stuff' in piloting," Yeager tells us, "then it is experience."

And yet, this proponent of the plateau, this traveler on the endless path, is also a man who speaks with wicked delight about "exploring the edges of the envelope." The night before he was scheduled to make a faster-than-sound flight for the first time in history, Yeager fell off a horse during a wild twilight ride and seriously sprained his shoulder. This injury would make it impossible for him to close the hatch on the X-1 rocket plane in the normal manner after he was loaded into it from the mother ship at 20,000 feet. Undaunted, he took along a broom handle so that he could close the door with his other hand—then went on to push through the sound barrier despite his injury.

The trick here is not only to test the edges of the envelope, but also to walk the fine line between endless, goalless practice and those alluring goals that appear along the way. At our dojo, we present aikido, first of all, as an endless path. But we also have periodic examinations that are rigorous, challenging, and sometimes quite dramatic. The exam for first-degree black belt is, in particular, a rite of passage. The candidate faces a three- to six-months-long period leading up to the exam, which becomes not only an intensive cram course in advanced techniques but also a physical and psychological trial by fire. During this ordeal, no personal flaw, no secret idiosyncracy, is likely to remain hidden. If all goes well, the exam itself becomes an expression not of ego but of essence, a climactic and transcendent moment in a long journey. But the journey is what counts. In the words of the ancient Eastern adage: "Before enlightenment, chop wood and carry water. After enlightenment, chop wood and carry water." The new black belt is expected to be on the mat the next day, ready to take the first fall.

Playing the edge is a balancing act. It demands the awareness to know when you're pushing yourself beyond safe limits. In this awareness, the man or woman on the path of mastery sometimes makes a conscious decision to do just that. We see this clearly in running, a sport so pure, so explicit that everything is likely to come quickly into full view. Running fast and hard almost always demands playing the edge, and it can't be denied that runners and would-be runners should be offered safe and sensible programs and warned against the dangers and pitfalls of their practice. Those who wish to run for specific, practical benefits—weight control, stress reduction, a healthy heart—must be given their due, but to limit the dialogue to such practical considerations is to demean the human spirit. Many people run not to lose weight but to loosen the chains of a mechanized culture, not to postpone death but to savor life. For those runners, the admonitions of critics who warn against the dangers of the sport are moot; they run quite consciously, as informed, consenting adults, to exceed their previous limits and to press the edges of the possible, whether this means completing their first circuit of a four-hundred-meter track without walking, or fighting for victory in a triathlon, as in an episode recounted in *American Medical News*.

> Few moments in sports history have so poignantly captured the agony of defeat as when twenty-three-year-old Julie Moss was leading the women's division of the twenty-six-mile marathon on Hawaii's Ironman Triathlon World Championship.
>
> With only one hundred yards left between her and the finish, Moss fell to her knees. She then rose, ran a few more yards, and collapsed again. As TV cameras rolled, she lost control of her bodily functions. She got up again, ran, fell, and then started crawling. Passed by the second-place runner, she crawled across the finish line, stretched out her arm, and passed out.
>
> Jim McKay of ABC Sports called it "heroic . . . one of the greatest moments in the history of televised sport." Gilbert Lang, M.D., an orthopedic surgeon at Roseville (California) Commu-

nity Hospital and a longtime endurance runner,
calls it "stupid—very nearly fatal."

Both Lang and McKay are right: it was stupid and
heroic. Surely no runner should be encouraged to go
so near the edge of death. But what type of world
would it be, how meager and pale, without such he-
roics? Perhaps there would be no human world at
all, for there must have been countless times before
the dawn of history when primitive hunters in pursuit of prey gave all of themselves in this way so that
members of their bands, our distant ancestors, could
live. People such as Julie Moss run for all of us, re-
affirming our humanity, our very existence. And
there is reason to believe that most of the people we
know as masters share her stupid, heroic desire to
use herself to the limit, to finish at all cost, to attain
the unattainable.

But before you can even consider playing this
edge, there must be many years of instruction, practice, surrender, and intentionality. And afterwards?
More training, more time on the plateau: the never-
ending path again.

 **PART THREE**

TOOLS FOR
MASTERY

Introduction

As the moment of departure draws near, it's time to get down to some specifics. How can you avoid backsliding? Where will you get the energy for your journey? What pitfalls will you encounter along the path? How can you apply mastery to the commonplace things of life? What should you pack for the journey?

Here are some travelers' tips, some parting gifts, and then—bon voyage!

Chapter 10

Why Resolutions Fail—and What to Do About It

You resolve to make a change for the better in your life. It could be any significant change, but let's say it involves getting on the path of mastery, developing a regular practice. You tell your friends about it. You put your resolution in writing. You actually make the change. It works. It feels good. You're happy about it. Your friends are happy about it. *Your life is better.* Then you backslide.

Why? Are you some kind of slob who has no will-power? Not necessarily. Backsliding is a universal experience. Every one of us resists significant change, no matter whether it's for the worse or for the better. Our body, brain, and behavior have a built-in tendency to stay the same within rather narrow limits, and to snap back when changed—and it's a very good thing they do.

Just think about it: if your body temperature

moved up or down by 10 percent, you'd be in big trouble. The same thing applies to your blood-sugar level and to any number of other functions of your body. This condition of equilibrium, this resistance to change, is called homeostasis. It characterizes all self-regulating systems, from a bacterium to a frog to a human individual to a family to an organization to an entire culture—and it applies to psychological states and behavior as well as to physical functioning.

The simplest example of homeostasis can be found in your home heating system. The thermostat on the wall senses the room temperature; when the temperature on a winter's day drops below the level you've set, the thermostat sends an electrical signal that turns the heater on. The heater completes the loop by sending heat to the room in which the thermostat is located. When the room temperature reaches the level you've set, the thermostat sends an electrical signal back to the heater, turning it off, thus maintaining homeostasis.

Keeping a room at the right temperature takes only one feedback loop. Keeping even the simplest single-celled organism alive and well takes thousands. And maintaining a human being in a state of homeostasis takes billions of interweaving electrochemical signals pulsing in the brain, rushing along nerve fibers, coursing through the bloodstream.

One example: each of us has about 150,000 tiny

thermostats in the form of nerve endings close to the surface of the skin that are sensitive to the loss of heat from our bodies, and another sixteen thousand or so a little deeper in the skin that alert us to the entry of heat from without. An even more sensitive thermostat resides in the hypothalamus at the base of the brain, close to branches of the main artery that brings blood from the heart to the head. This thermostat can pick up even the tiniest change of temperature in the blood. When you start getting cold, these thermostats signal the sweat glands, pores, and small blood vessels near the surface of the body to close down. Glandular activity and muscle tension cause you to shiver in order to produce more heat, and your senses send a very clear message to your brain, leading you to keep moving, to put on more clothes, to cuddle closer to someone, to seek shelter, or to build a fire.

Homeostasis in social groups brings additional feedback loops into play. Families stay stable by means of instruction, exhortation, punishment, privileges, gifts, favors, signs of approval and affection, and even by means of extremely subtle body language and facial expressions. Social groups larger than the family add various types of feedback systems. A national culture, for example, is held together by the legislative process, law enforcement, education, the popular arts, sports and games, economic rewards that favor certain types of activity, and by a complex web of mores, prestige markers, celebrity role modeling, and style that relies largely on the media as a national nervous system. Although we might think that our culture is mad for the new, the predominant function of all this—as with the feedback loops in your body—is the survival of things as they are.

The problem is, homeostasis works to keep things as they are even if they aren't very good. Let's say, for instance, that for the last twenty years—ever since high school, in fact—you've been almost entirely sedentary. Now most of your friends are working out, and you figure that if you can't beat the fitness revolution, you'll join it. Buying the tights and running shoes is fun, and so are the first few steps as you start jogging on the high school track near your house. Then, about a third of the way around the first lap, something terrible happens. Maybe you're suddenly sick to your stomach. Maybe you're dizzy. Maybe there's a strange, panicky feeling in your chest. Maybe you're going to die.

No, you're going to die. What's more, the particular sensations you're feeling probably aren't significant in themselves. What you're really getting is a homeostatic alarm signal—bells clanging, lights flashing. *Warning! Warning! Significant changes in res-*

piration, heart rate, metabolism. Whatever you're doing, stop doing it immediately.

Homeostasis, remember, doesn't distinguish between what you would call change for the better and change for the worse. It resists *all* change. After twenty years without exercise, your body regards a sedentary style of life as "normal"; the beginning of a change for the better is interpreted as a threat. So you walk slowly back to your car, figuring you'll look around for some other revolution to join.

Take another case, involving a family of five. The father happens to be an alcoholic who goes on a binge every six to eight weeks. During the time he's drinking, and for several days afterward, the family is in an uproar. It's nothing new. These periodic uproars have become, in fact, the normal state of things. Then, for one reason or another, the father stops drinking. You'd think that everyone in the family would be happy, and they are—for a while. But homeostasis has strange and sneaky ways of striking back. There's a pretty good chance that within a very few months some other family member (say, a teenage son) will do something (say, get caught dealing drugs) to create just the type of uproar the father's binges previously triggered. Without wise professional counsel, the members of this family won't realize that the son, unknowingly, has simply taken the father's place to keep the family system in the condition that has become stable and "normal."

No need here to count the ways that organizations and cultures resist change and backslide when change does occur. Just let it be said that the resistance here (as in other cases) is proportionate to the size and speed of the change, not to whether the change is a favorable or unfavorable one. If an organizational or cultural reform meets tremendous resistance, it is because it's either a tremendously bad idea or a tremendously good idea. Trivial change, bureaucratic meddling, is much easier to accept, and that's one reason why you see so much of it. In the same way, the talkier forms of psychotherapy are acceptable, at least to some degree, perhaps because they sometimes change nothing very much except the patient's ability to talk about his or her problems. But none of this is meant to condemn homeostasis. We want our minds and bodies and organizations to hold together. We want that paycheck to arrive on schedule. In order to survive, we need stability.

Still, change does occur. Individuals change. Families change. Organizations and entire cultures change. Homeostats are reset, even though the process might cause a certain amount of anxiety, pain, and upset. The questions are: How do you deal with homeostasis? How do you make change for the better easier? How do you make it last?

These questions rise to great importance when you embark on the path of mastery. Say that after years of hacking around in your career, you decide to approach it in terms of the principles of mastery. Your whole life obviously will change, and thus you'll have to deal with homeostasis. But even if you should begin applying mastery to pursuits such as gardening or tennis, which might seem less than central to your existence, the effects of the change might ripple out to touch almost everything you do. Realizing significantly more of your potential in almost anything can change you in many ways. And however much you enjoy and profit from the change, you'll probably meet with homeostasis sooner or later. You might experience homeostatic alarm signals in the form of physical or psychological symptoms. You might unknowingly sabotage your own best efforts. You might get resistance from family, friends, and co-workers. And you can consider yourself fortunate indeed if you don't find yourself on that old, familiar slide back to the ways of the Dabbler, or the Obsessive, or the Hacker.

Ultimately, you'll have to decide if you really do want to spend the time and effort it takes to get on and stay on the path. If you do, here are five guidelines that might help. While these guidelines are focused on mastery, they could also be applied to any change in your life.

1. Be aware of the way homeostasis works. This might be the most important guideline of all. Expect resistance and backlash. Realize that when the alarm bells start ringing, it doesn't necessarily mean you're sick or crazy or lazy or that you've made a bad decision in embarking on the journey of mastery. In fact, you might take these signals as an indication that your life is definitely changing—just what you've wanted. Of course, it might be that you *have* started something that's not right for you; only you can decide. But in any case, don't panic and give up at the first sign of trouble.

You might also expect resistance from friends and family and co-workers. (Homeostasis, as we've seen, applies to social systems as well as individuals.) Say you used to struggle out of bed at 7:30 and barely drag yourself to work at 9:00. Now that you're on a path of mastery, you're up at 6:00 for a three-mile run, and in the office, charged with energy, at 8:30. You might figure that your co-workers would be overjoyed, but don't be too sure. And when you get home, still raring to go, do you think that your family will welcome the change? Maybe. Bear in mind that an entire system has to change when any part of it changes. So don't be surprised if some of the people you love start covertly or overtly undermining your self-improvement. It's not that they wish you harm, it's just homeostasis at work.

2. *Be willing to negotiate with your resistance to change.* So what should you do when you run into resistance, when the red lights flash and the alarm bells ring? Well, you don't back off, and you don't bull your way through. Negotiation is the ticket to successful long-term change in everything from increasing your running speed to transforming your organization. The long-distance runner working for a faster time on a measured course negotiates with homeostasis by using pain not as an adversary but as the best possible guide to performance. The change-oriented manager keeps his or her eyes and ears open for signs of dissatisfaction or dislocation, then plays the edge of discontent, the inevitable escort of transformation.

The fine art of playing the edge in this case involves a willingness to take one step back for every two forward, sometimes vice versa. It also demands a determination to keep pushing, but not without awareness. Simply turning off your awareness to the warnings deprives you of guidance and risks damaging the system. Simply pushing your way through despite the warning signals increases the possibility of backsliding.

You can never be sure exactly where the resistance

will pop up. A feeling of anxiety? Psychosomatic complaints? A tendency toward self-sabotage? Squabbles with family, friends, or fellow workers? None of the above? Stay alert. Be prepared for serious negotiations.

3. Develop a support system. You can do it alone, but it helps a great deal to have other people with whom you can share the joys and perils of the change you're making. The best support system would involve people who have gone through or are going through a similar process, people who can tell their own stories of change and listen to yours, people who will brace you up when you start to backslide and encourage you when you don't. The path of mastery, fortunately, almost always fosters social groupings. In his seminal book *Homo Ludens: A Study of the Play Element in Culture,* Johan Huizinga comments upon the tendency of sports and games to bring people together. The play community, he points out, is likely to continue even after the game is over, inspired by "the feeling of being 'apart together' in an exceptional situation, of sharing something important, of mutually withdrawing from the rest of the world and rejecting the usual norms." The same can be said about many other pursuits, whether or not they are formally known as sports—arts and crafts, hunting, fishing, yoga, Zen, the professions, "the office."

And what if your quest for mastery is a lonely one? What if you can find no fellow voyagers on that particular path? At the least, you can let the people close to you know what you're doing, and ask for their support.

4. Follow a regular practice. People embarking on any type of change can gain stability and comfort through practicing some worthwhile activity on a more or less regular basis, not so much for the sake of achieving an external goal as simply for its own sake. A traveler on the path of mastery is again fortunate, for practice in this sense (as I've said more than once) is the foundation of the path itself. The circumstances are particularly happy in case you've already established a regular practice in something else before facing the challenge and change of beginning a new one. It's easier to start applying the principles of mastery to your profession or your primary relationship if you've already established a regular morning exercise program. Practice is a habit, and any regular practice provides a sort of underlying homeostasis, a stable base during the instability of change.

5. Dedicate yourself to lifelong learning. We tend to forget that learning is much more than book learning. To learn is to change. Education, whether it involves books, body, or behavior, is a process that changes the learner. It doesn't have to end at college graduation or at age forty or sixty or eighty, and the best learning of all involves learning how to learn— that is, to change. The lifelong learner is essentially one who has learned to deal with homeostasis, simply because he or she is doing it all the time. The Dabbler, Obsessive, and Hacker are all learners in their own fashion, but lifelong learning is the special province of those who travel the path of mastery, the path that never ends.

Chapter 11

Getting Energy for Mastery

If you think you simply don't have the time or the energy to dedicate yourself to mastery, consider the old adage that if you want to get something done, ask a busy person to do it. Most of us know at least one of those prodigies of energy who get far more than their share of the world's work and play accomplished. When we stop to think about it, in fact, almost all of us can bring to mind periods when we, too, were bursting with energy; when no mountain seemed too high for us; when the boundaries between work and play blurred and finally disappeared. Remember when you could barely keep your eyes open in class, yet were totally awake and alert during hours of tough after-school sports practice? And how about that rush of energy at the beginning of a love affair, or during a challenging job situation, or at the approach of danger?

A human being is the kind of machine that wears out from *lack* of use. There are limits, of course, and we do need healthful rest and relaxation, but for the most part we gain energy by using energy. Often the best remedy for physical weariness is thirty minutes of aerobic exercise. In the same way, mental and spiritual lassitude is often cured by decisive action or the clear intention to act. We learn in high school physics that kinetic energy is measured in terms of motion. The same thing is true of human energy: it comes into existence through use. You can't hoard it. As Frederich S. (Fritz) Perls, founder of Gestalt therapy, used to say, "I don't want to be saved, I want to be *spent.*" It might well be that all of us possess enormous stores of potential energy, more than we could ever hope to use.

If this is so, then why do we so often feel drained, unable to drag ourselves to the simplest task? Why do we leave those letters unanswered, that leaky faucet unrepaired? Why do we resist our own most constructive and creative impulses and squander our best energy on busywork? Why do we sit for hours in the babbling bath of television while life's abundant opportunities drift past unseen?

It starts in earliest childhood. Watch an unfettered eighteen-month-old for a couple of hours. This miniature prodigy of energy has an important job (call it raw, unadulterated learning), and he ruthlessly exploits everything in his environment, that he can see, hear, taste, smell, and feel to get that job done. Some restraints must be imposed, but we tend to impose far more than safety requires. After all, we adults have already forfeited much of our energy and are easily exhausted. So we might say, "Why can't you be still?" or "I can't stand that yammering for one more second." We might try angry commands, physical restraint, or—God help us—physical punishment. More likely, we'll put the learning process on hold by parking the learner in front of the television set, no matter what's on. There! That's better! Now the kid's as lethargic as we are.

In school the child gets even worse news: learning is dull. There's only one right answer to every question, and you'd better learn that answer by sitting still and listening passively, not *doing* anything. The conventional classroom setup, with twenty to thirty-five kids forced to do the same thing at the same time, makes individual initiative and exploration nearly impossible. There's certainly little space for the playful exuberance that accompanies high energy. Six-year-old Johnny wants to sing a song to the class. "Not now, Johnny. We have work to do." Or worse: "Don't be *silly,* Johnny." That teacher's voice still resonates in forty-year-old Johnny's subconscious whenever he's tempted to be spontaneous.

With   maddening   inefficiency,   conventional

schooling finally manages to teach reading and writing and figuring and a smattering of facts, but the operative words are too often *don't, no,* and *wrong.* The fundamental learning is negative. "It is in fact nothing short of a miracle," Albert Einstein wrote, "that the modern methods of instruction have not yet entirely strangled the holy curiosity of inquiry. . . . It is a very grave mistake to think that the enjoyment of seeing and searching can be promoted by means of coercion and sense of duty."

But it isn't just school. Peer groups at every stage of life exert a leveling influence. Conformity is valued. High energy is feared as a threat to conformity. And, of course, it often is. There's something frightening about the unbridled release of human energy. The psychopath, for example, is one who has failed to internalize society's restraints. Sometimes possessing unusual charm and persuasiveness, always lacking conscience and remorse, he is able to direct seemingly superhuman amounts of energy to his goals, which tend to the short-term and self-serving.

This dark energy both dismays and fascinates us. We find ourselves strangely attracted to the man in the black hat, to villains and rogues of all types, precisely because they so blatantly express what we won't even acknowledge in ourselves. And look at the daily news, at the rapacious preachers, the phony gurus, the larcenous financiers, the organizers of shadowy armies and arms deals—all of them short on scruples and long on passionate intensity. We have reason to be wary of the driven personality, the zealot. No wonder society wants to "socialize" us, to squash our energy.

That's the downside, but there's also that legion of thoughtful and responsible people who have some-how retained their native energy and know how to put it to work for their benefit and ours. The energy they manifest is to a large extent available to all of us. If we could tap as little as an added 10 percent of this vast resource, our lives would be significantly altered. Here's how to get started:

1. Maintain physical fitness. We all know physi-cally fit people who sit around shuffling papers all day. And we also know those energy demons who still maintain that when the urge to exercise comes over them, they simply lie down until it passes. But, all things being equal, physical fitness contributes enormously to energy in every aspect of our lives. We might also suspect that, all things again being equal, those people who feel good about themselves, who are in touch with nature and their own bodies, are more likely to use their energy for the good of this planet and its people than those who live sed-entary, unhealthy lives.

2. *Acknowledge the negative and accentuate the positive.* The power of positive thinking informs everything from pop-preacher Norman Vincent Peale's book of the same name to Skinnerian psychology to the newest management-training seminars. Optimism gets regularly trashed by intellectuals as well as by self-proclaimed "tough-minded" journalists and commentators, but numerous studies show that people with a positive outlook on life suffer far less sickness than those who see the world in negative terms.

They also have more energy.

Tom Peters, author of *In Search of Excellence,* and perhaps the nation's top management consultant, speaks of "an almost spooky similarity of language" among the managers of America's most successful companies. To a man and a woman, they stress the value of a positive attitude and the effectiveness of praise and other forms of positive feedback. "The most successful managers," Peters told me, "are those who are unwilling to tolerate the negative stuff." Peters cites one study's findings that very successful people had had "an obnoxiously high level of praise piled on them in childhood—praise to the point of embarrassment. It seems you can hardly overdo it."

Is it possible to be *too* positive? Only if you deny the existence of negative factors, of situations in your life and in the world at large that need correcting.

Some Eastern philosophies as well as certain Western religions and quasi-religions do just that. Their insistence that evils and ills are nothing more than illusion comforts the converted but often leads to a harmful denial of personal reality and a callousness toward the injustices in the world. Generally, denial inhibits energy, while realistic acknowledgment of the truth releases it.

Even serious blows in life can give you extra energy by knocking you off dead center, shaking you out of your lethargy—*but not if you deny the blows are real.* Acknowledging the negative doesn't mean sniveling; it means facing the truth and then moving on. Simply describing what's wrong with your life to a good friend is likely to make you feel better and more energetic.

Once you've dealt with the negative, you're free to concentrate on the best in yourself. Whenever possible, avoid teachers and supervisors who are highly critical in a negative sense. Telling people what they're doing wrong while ignoring what they're doing right reduces their energy. When it's your turn to teach or supervise or give advice, you might try the following approach: "Here's what I like about what you're doing, and here's how you might improve it."

3. Try telling the truth. "There's nothing more energizing to a corporation than for people to start telling one another truth,'' says Dr. Will Schutz, who popularized truth-telling encounter groups in the 1960s and is now a corporate consultant. "One of the first results we got after our sessions with corporate executives was that their meetings were shorter than before. One company reported that hour-and-a-half meetings now take twenty minutes. 'We just say what we want to say. We don't have to spend a lot of time and energy *not* saying something.' Lies and secrets are poison in organizations—people's energy is devoted to deceiving and hiding and remembering who it is you don't want to tell what to. When people start telling the truth, you see almost immediate reductions in mistakes and increases in productivity.''

Truth-telling works best when it involves revealing your own feelings, not when used to insult others and to get your own way. All in all, it has a lot going for it—risk, challenge, excitement, and the release of all of that energy.

4. Honor but don't indulge your own dark side. God knows how much energy we have locked up in the submerged part of our personality, in what Carl Jung calls the shadow. Poet and storyteller Robert Bly gives a modern setting to Jung's ideas in his book *A Little Book on the Human Shadow*. The young child, Bly tells us, can be visualized as a lively ball of energy that radiates in all directions. But the parents don't like certain parts of the ball. In order to keep the parents' love, the child puts the parts of him that they don't like in an invisible bag that he drags behind him. "By the time we go to school," Bly writes, "the bag is quite large. Then our teachers have their say: 'Good children don't get angry over such little things.' So we take our anger and put it in the bag." By age twenty, he maintains, only a thin slice of our original energy is left.

But the energy we've hidden away can still be available to us. And putting those forbidden parts of our personality to work doesn't involve indulging ourselves and literally acting out the submerged part. Anger, for instance, contains a great deal of energy. If we've repressed that emotion so effectively that we can't even feel it, we obviously can't use the energy that goes along with it in any conscious, constructive way. But if we take our anger out of the bag simply to indulge it, if we let anger become a knee-jerk response, we dissipate its considerable power. There are times when it's appropriate to express anger, but there's also the possibility of taking the fervid energy of indignation, even of rage, and putting it to work for positive purposes. In other words, when you feel your anger rising, you can choose to go and work furiously on a favorite project, or to transmute the energy beneath your anger to fuel that you can use on your journey of mastery.

We'll enjoy a much more energetic world when society stops forcing us to put so much of ourselves into that invisible bag. Until then, we can note that the prodigies of energy whom we admire are precisely those people who know how to utilize the blazing energy that flows from that which has been called dark.

5. Set your priorities. Before you can use your potential energy, you have to decide what you're going to do with it. And in making any choice, you face a monstrous fact: to move in one direction, you must forgo all others. To choose one goal is to forsake a very large number of other possible goals. A friend of mine, twenty-nine and still looking for a cause, a purpose in life, said, "Our generation has been raised on the idea of keeping your options open. But if you keep all your options open, you can't do a damned thing." It's a problem: How can any one option, any one goal, match up to the possibilities contained in all others?

This troubling equation applies to everything from lifetime goals to what you're going to do in the next ten minutes. Should you clean out that messy closet or start reading that new book or write that letter? An affluent, consumer-oriented way of life multiplies the choices that face you. Television makes it even more complicated. By offering endless possibilities, it tempts you to choose none, to sit staring in endless wonder, to become comatose. Indecision leads to inaction, which leads to low energy, depression, despair.

Ultimately, liberation comes through the acceptance of limits. You can't do everything, but you can do one thing, and then another and another. In terms of energy, it's better to make a wrong choice than none at all. You might begin by listing your priorities—for the day, for the week, for the month, for a lifetime. Start modestly. List everything you want to do today or tomorrow. Set priorities by dividing the items into A, B, and C categories. At the least, accomplish the A items. Try the same thing with long-term goals. Priorities do shift, and you can change them at any time, but simply getting them down in black and white adds clarity to your life, and clarity creates energy.

6. Make commitments. Take action. The journey of mastery is ultimately goalless; you take the journey for the sake of the journey itself. But, as I've pointed out, there are interim goals along the way, the first of which is simply starting the journey. And there's nothing quite so immediately energizing on any journey as the intermediate goal of a tough, firm deadline—as is well known to anyone who has faced an opening-night curtain, a business-deal closing date, or a definite press time for an article or book. At our aikido school, a notice is placed on the bulletin board four times a year asking qualified students to sign up for ranking exams. Some students sign immediately, while others wait until a few days before the exam. It's instructive to watch the immediate surge of clarity and energy during training that comes from the simplest act of writing one's name on a notice. Those who sign late suffer from having less time in which to enjoy the energy that flows from commitment.

The gift of an externally imposed deadline isn't always available. Sometimes you need to set your own. But you have to take it seriously. One way to do this is to make it public. Tell people who are important in your life. The firmer the deadline, the harder it is to break, and the more energy it confers. Above all else, move and keep moving. Don't go off half cocked. Take time for wise planning, but don't take forever. "Whatever you can do, or dream you can— begin it," Goethe wrote. "Boldness has genius, power, and magic in it."

7. *Get on the path of mastery and stay on it.* Over the long haul, there's nothing like the path of mastery to lead you to an energetic life. A regular practice not only elicits energy but tames it. Without the

firm underpinnings of a practice, deadlines can produce violent swings between frantic activity and collapse. On the master's journey, you can learn to put things in perspective, to keep the flow of energy going during low moments as well as high. You also learn that you can't hoard energy; you can't build it up by not using it. Adequate rest is, of course, a part of the master's journey, but, unaccompanied by positive action, rest may only depress you.

It might well be, in fact, that much of the world's depression and discontent, and perhaps even a good share of the pervasive malaise that leads to crime and war, can ultimately be traced to our unused energy, our untapped potential. People whose energy is flowing don't need to take a drug, commit a crime, or go to war in order to feel fully awake and alive. There's enough constructive, creative work for everybody, with plenty left over. All of us can increase our energy, starting now.

 **Chapter 12**

Pitfalls Along the Path

It's easy to get on the path of mastery. The real challenge lies in staying on it. The most dedicated traveler will find pitfalls as well as rewards along the way. You probably can't avoid them all, but it helps to know they're there. Here are thirteen you might run into on your journey.

1. Conflicting way of life. The path of mastery doesn't exist in a vacuum. It wends its way through a landscape of other obligations, pleasures, relationships. The traveler whose main path of mastery coincides with career and livelihood is fortunate; others must find space and time outside regular working hours for a preferred practice that brings mastery but not a living wage. The trick here is to be realistic: will you actually be able to balance job and path? But don't despair, we all possess great stores of unused

133

energy (see Chapter Eleven). And as for time, how about those seven hours a day (the national average) spent watching television. There's also the matter of family and friends. Do you have their support for what you're doing? Especially, do you have your spouse's support? "Never marry a person," psychologist Nathaniel Brandon tells his clients, "who is not a friend of your excitement." The point is, when things aren't going well on your path of mastery, don't forget to check out the rest of your life. Then consider the possibility that the rest of your life can be lived in terms of mastery principles.

2. Obsessive goal orientation. As pointed out numerous times in this book, the desire of most people today for quick, sure, and highly visible results is perhaps the deadliest enemy of mastery. It's fine to have ambitious goals, but the best way of reaching them is to cultivate modest expectations at every step along the way. When you're climbing a mountain, in other words, be aware that the peak is ahead, but don't keep looking up at it. Keep your eyes on the path. And when you reach the top of the mountain, as the Zen saying goes, keep on climbing.

3. Poor instruction. You've already read about the importance of good instruction and how to recognize bad instruction (see Chapter Five). To repeat a couple of points: surrender to your teacher, but only as a teacher, not as a guru. Don't bounce from one teacher to another, but don't stick with a situation that's not working, just out of inertia. And remember: the ultimate responsibility for your getting good instruction lies not with your teacher but with you.

4. *Lack of competitiveness.* Competition provides spice in life as well as in sports; it's only when the spice becomes the entire diet that the player gets sick. Competition can provide motivation. It can also help hold games and other enterprises together; to compete with someone, you have to agree to run on the same track. Take competition as an opportunity to hone your hard-won skills to a fine edge. Failing to play wholeheartedly with a will to win degrades the game and insults the opponent. Winning is an essential element in the journey, but it isn't the only thing. Winning graciously and losing with equal grace are the marks of a master.

5. *Overcompetitiveness.* The would-be master who thinks about nothing but winning is sure to lose in the long run. The statement "Winning isn't everything, it's the only thing" is one of the greatest of hoaxes. Think about it: if winning is the *only* thing, then practice, discipline, conditioning, and character are *nothing.* It's said that winning is a habit—but so

is losing. The "number one" criterion, with its attendant overcompetitiveness, creates far more losers than winners. Who knows how many potential Olympic medalists have turned away from sports because of youth-league coaches who preach that the purpose of life lies in beating the school on the other side of town, and that it doesn't matter how you play the game, just so you win.

6. *Laziness.* Laziness can be analyzed in psychiatric terms—such as resistance and dependence—but it might be more useful just to get right down to the word itself, which is defined as "Disinclined to action or exertion; averse to labor, indolent; idle; slothful." The bad news is that laziness will knock you off the path. The good news is that the path is the best possible cure for laziness. Courage.

7. *Injuries.* If your path is a physical one, and if you're like most of us, you'll probably encounter injuries somewhere along the way. Minor ones come with the territory. There are also serious injuries, which can take you off the path temporarily or even permanently. Except in heavy-contact sports, most of these serious injuries are probably avoidable. People get hurt because of obsessive goal orientation, because they get ahead of themselves, because they lose consciousness of what's going on in their own

bodies, in the here and now. The best way of achieving a goal is to be fully present. Surpassing previous limits involves negotiating with your body, not ignoring or overriding its messages. Negotiation involves awareness. Avoiding serious injury is less a matter of being cautious than of being conscious. All of this is also true to some extent of mental and emotional as well as physical injuries.

8. Drugs. Drugs can give you the illusion of getting the immediate success this culture is always promising you. Travelers on the fast track can use drugs to experience climactic upward surges without spending any time on the plateau. At first, it might seem to work, but regular use leads inevitably to disaster. If you're on drugs, you're not on the path.

9. Prizes and medals. Excessive use of external motivation can slow and even stop your journey to mastery. Studies show that rewarding schoolchildren by giving them gold stars initially speeds up their learning, but their progress soon levels off, even if you increase the number of stars. When you stop giving stars, their progress falls to a level lower than that of matched groups of children who got no stars in the first place. A report on the physiological limits of running speed shows that the major factor stopping the improvement of a champion runner's speed is setting a record or winning an important medal. "The champions stop not at a given speed but when they set a record," authors Henry W. Ryder, Harry Jay Carr, and Paul Herget wrote in the June 1976 *Scientific American.* "Succeeding champions do the same. They telescope in their relatively short racing lives all the achievements of the great runners of the past and then stop with a gold medal just as their predecessors did. Since it is the medal and not the speed that stops them, the speeds they reach cannot be considered in any way the ultimate physiological limit." Perhaps we'll never know how far the path can go, how much a human being can truly achieve, until we realize that the ultimate reward is not a gold medal but the path itself.

10. Vanity. It's possible that one of the reasons you got on the path of mastery was to look good. But to learn something new of any significance, you have to be willing to look foolish. Even after years of practice, you still take pratfalls. When a Most Valuable Player candidate misjudges a ball and falls on his duff, he does it in the sight of millions. You should be willing to do it before your teacher and a few friends or fellow students. If you're always thinking about appearances, you can never attain the state of concentration that's necessary for effective learning and top performance.

11. Dead seriousness. Without laughter, the rough and rocky places on the path might be too painful to bear. Humor not only lightens your load, it also broadens your perspective. To be deadly serious is to suffer tunnel vision. To be able to laugh at yourself clears the vision. When choosing fellow voyagers, beware of grimness, self-importance, and the solemn eye.

12. Inconsistency. Consistency of practice is the mark of the master. Continuity of time and place (where this is feasible) can establish a rhythm that buoys you up, carries you along. There is even value in repeating favorite rituals before, during, and after practice. Psychologist Mihaly Csikszentmihalyi, who has studied a state of happy concentration called "flow," points out that some surgeons wash their hands and put on their gowns in precisely the same way before each operation, thus stripping their minds of outside concerns and focusing their attention fully on the task at hand. Inconsistency not only loses you practice time, but makes everything more difficult when you do get around to practicing. But if you should happen to miss a few sessions, don't use that as an excuse to quit entirely. The path of mastery takes many twists and turns and calls for a certain flexibility of strategy and action. Consistency is of the essence, but a foolish consistency, as Ralph Waldo Emerson tells us, "is the hobgoblin of little minds."

13. Perfectionism. In a way, it's a pity that technology has brought so many masterful performances into our homes. "Twenty-four hours of world-class orchestras" is what the local classical music station promises me. And these performances are not only meticulously rehearsed, but recorded repeatedly, with the very best passages spliced together, and the entire recording electronically enhanced. Traveling exhibits bring the works of Van Gogh, Degas, Gauguin, and Manet to our local art museums. And on television we can watch top athletes, dancers, ice skaters, singers, actors, comics, and pundits, all giving us their best. Compared to this, how can we even talk about mastery? Then there are those of us who are simply self-critical. Even without comparing ourselves to the world's greatest, we set such high standards for ourselves that neither we nor anyone else could ever meet them—and nothing is more destructive to creativity than this. We fail to realize that mastery is not about perfection. It's about a process, a journey. The master is the one who stays on the path day after day, year after year. The master is the one who is willing to try, and fail, and try again, for as long as he or she lives.

Chapter 13

Mastering the Commonplace

Our preoccupation with goals, results, and the quick fix has separated us from our own experiences. To put it more starkly, it has robbed us of countless hours of the time of our lives. We awaken in the morning and hurry to get dressed. (Getting dressed doesn't count.) We hurry to eat breakfast so that we can leave for work. (Eating breakfast doesn't count.) We hurry to get to work. (Getting to work doesn't count.) Maybe work will be interesting and satisfying and we won't have to simply endure it while waiting for lunchtime to come. And maybe lunch will bring a warm, intimate meeting, with fascinating conversation. But maybe not.

In any case, there are all of those chores that most of us can't avoid: cleaning, straightening, raking leaves, shopping for groceries, driving the children to various activities, preparing food, washing dishes, washing the car, commuting, performing the routine, repetitive aspects of our jobs. This is the "in-between time," the stuff we have to take care of before getting on to the things that count. But if you stop to think about it, most of life is "in between." When goal orientation comes to dominate our thoughts, little that seems to really count is left. During the usual nonplayoff year, the actual playing time for a National Football League team is sixteen hours. For the players, does this mean that the other 8,744 hours of the year are "in between"? Does all time take its significance only in terms of the product, the bottom line? And if winning, as the saying goes, is the *only* thing, does that mean that even the climactic hours achieve their worth merely through victory?

There's another way of thinking about it. Zen practice is ostensibly organized around periods of sitting in meditation and chanting. Yet every Zen master will tell you that building a stone wall or washing dishes is essentially no different from formal meditation. The quality of a Zen student's practice is defined just as much by how he or she sweeps the courtyard as by how he or she sits in meditation. Could we apply this way of thinking to less esoteric situations? Could all of us reclaim the lost hours of our lives by making everything—the commonplace along with the extraordinary—a part of our practice?

Driving as High Art

Take driving, for instance. Say you need to drive ten miles to visit a friend. You might consider the trip itself as in-between time, something to get over with. Or you could take it as an opportunity for the practice of mastery. In that case, you would approach your car in a state of full awareness, conscious of the time of day, the temperature, the wind speed and direction, the angle of the sun, or the presence of rain, snow, or sleet. Let this awareness extend to your own mental, physical, and emotional condition. Take a moment to walk around the car and check its external condition, especially that of the tires. Make sure the windshield and windows are clean enough to provide good visibility. Check the oil and other fluid levels if it's time to do so.

Open the door and get in the driver's seat, performing the next series of actions as a ritual: fastening the seat belt, adjusting the seat and the rearview mirrors, checking the pressure on the brake pedal and the play of the steering wheel. Then, before starting the engine, relax and take a deep breath. Pay special attention to releasing any tension in your neck, shoulders, and abdomen. Lean back so that your back makes firm contact with the seat back, as if you're sinking *into* it. Become aware of the pressure of your buttocks and legs on the seat itself; feel yourself merging with the seat, becoming one with the entire car.

Start the engine and attend carefully to its sounds and vibrations. Check all of the gauges; make sure there's plenty of fuel. Bring to mind any problems you've been having with the car lately and consider how this might affect your trip. As you begin moving, make a silent affirmation that you'll take responsibility for the space all around your vehicle at all times—the back and sides as well as the front—and that, insofar as possible, you'll drive in such a way as to avoid an accident, no matter what other cars might do.

Taking this short trip will afford you many opportunities for practicing mastery. We tend to downgrade driving as a skill simply because it's so common. Actually, maneuvering a car through varying conditions of weather, traffic, and road surface calls for an extremely high level of perception, concentration, coordination, and judgment. In the 1960s, UCLA brain researchers measured the brainwave activity of astronaut candidates practicing a moon landing in a simulator and also driving on a Los Angeles freeway. As it turned out, driving on the freeway occasioned more brain activity.

These are a few of the particularly exquisite skills offered every driver: anticipating the possible moves of all the cars in your field of action; entering a curve at the correct speed and accelerating slightly during the turn; braking smoothly and with a feeling of continuity rather than rushing up behind another car and slamming on the brakes; engaging the clutch on a stick shift with perfect synchrony; changing lanes on a busy freeway without discomforting other drivers; dealing gracefully with the unexpected.

Driving can be high art, finely balanced between long periods of seeming routine and brief moments of terrifying challenge, with the possibility of injury or death always waiting around the next corner. These considerations lend added weight to the need for mastery in driving. But your practice of far humbler skills can also gain from an application of mastery principles.

Household Rhythm

Take dishwashing, for example. You can perform that chore in a hurried and haphazard way, with your main goal being to get it behind you as quickly as possible. Or you can do it as a meditation, a dance. If you choose this option, take a moment to compose yourself before beginning. Briefly balance and center yourself (see Chapter Fourteen). Decide on the general sequence of your work, then begin. Maintain full awareness of each of your movements. Even though your hands are most directly involved, pay attention to the rest of your body, especially the feet, abdomen, shoulders, and back. Imagine that all of your movements are emanating from your physical center of mass, a point about an inch below your navel. Go for efficiency, elegance, and grace in your motions; avoid hasty shortcuts. Rather than thinking about getting the job finished and going on to something else, stay wholly focused on the moment, on the task at hand. Above all, don't hurry. You might discover that by not hurrying you'll finish the dishes sooner than would ordinarily be the case. The odds are good that you'll feel better at the end.

Life is filled with opportunities for practicing the inexorable, unhurried rhythm of mastery, which focuses on process rather than product, yet which, paradoxically, often ends up creating more and better products in a shorter time than does the hurried, excessively goal-oriented rhythm that has become standard in our society. Making this rhythm habitual takes practice. The canister vacuum cleaner is a particularly fiendish teacher in the quest for mastery of the commonplace. The snakelike vacuum tube and long power cord seem specifically designed to snag on every available object in the room. The canister seems obstinately determined either to bump into or get hung up on every piece of furniture. The attachment connected to the vacuum tube invariably seems the wrong one for the next task at hand. The power cord reaches its limit and has to be replugged at the most inconvenient moments.

Those of you who have managed to avoid vacuuming don't know what you're missing: an onerous chore, yes, but also a fine opportunity—no less taxing than balancing your books or getting the footnotes straight on your dissertation or working out a kink in your golf swing—for practicing some of the skills you'll need on the path. The person who can vacuum an entire house without once losing his or her composure, staying balanced, centered, and focused on the process rather than pressing impatiently for completion, is a person who knows something about mastery.

The Challenge of Relationships

On the level of personal experience, all of life is seamless, despite society's untiring efforts to break it up into compartments. The way we walk, talk to our children, and make love bears a significant relationship to the way we ski, study for a profession, or do our jobs. It's truly bizarre, when you stop to think about it, that we are sometimes quite willing to give full attention to developing our tennis game while leaving such "commonplace" things as relationships largely to chance.

The truth of the matter is that if you have to work

at a sport to achieve mastery, you also have to work, and generally work even more diligently, to achieve mastery in relationships. In both, there will be ups and downs and long periods on the plateau. And you'll eventually discover, in every significant area of your life, that the most important learning and development takes place during your time on the plateau. The same principles apply here as elsewhere. Note in the following paragraphs, for example, how the five keys to mastery can be applied to relationships.

Instruction. Some people sneer at the notion of counseling for couples, or books and tapes about better relationships. It's true that some of the counseling is vapid, and the language in some of the books and tapes can make you gag, but an intimate relationship can become insular before either partner knows it, and it's hard to solve every problem alone. If you're on the path of mastery, whether in sports or relationships or anything else, you'll invariably seek the best guidance available, whether it's a counselor, a book, or a sympathetic, unbiased friend. But shop around, choose carefully, get recommendations.

Practice. The sportsperson is willing to devote several concentrated sessions a week to a sport. Couples on the path of mastery might do at least that much, setting aside specific times just for the relationship, apart from children, friends, work, and the usual entertainments. But practice, as we've seen, goes beyond that, involving a certain steadfastness, an ability to take pleasure in the endless repetition of ordinary acts.

Surrender. The ability to surrender to your art is a mark of the master, whether the art is martial or marital. Can you let go of an outworn behavior pattern without knowing exactly what will replace it? Are you willing at times to yield totally on some long-standing dispute for the sake of growth and change in your relationship? The tricky part is learning to lose your ego without losing your balance. The stronger you are the more you can give of yourself. The more you give of yourself, the stronger you can be.

Intentionality. To cultivate a positive attitude is to take a large step on the path of mastery in relationships. In addition, mental toughness (the ability to focus on a problem or a long-term goal) combined with openness and imagination (the ability to see options and visualize desired states) can be applied to relationships as well as to sports, or anything else.

The Edge. The path of mastery is built on unrelenting practice, but it's also a place of adventure. A couple on the path stays open to experience and is willing to play new games, dance new dances together. Perhaps the greatest adventure of all is intimacy: the willingness to strip away one layer of reticence after another, and on certain occasions to live entirely in the moment, revealing everything and expecting nothing in return.

The point of this chapter is that the principles of mastery can guide you, whatever skill you seek to develop, whatever path you choose to walk. In the words of Chinese Zen master Layman P'ang (c. 740–808 A.D.):

> *My daily affairs are quite ordinary;*
> *but I'm in total harmony with them.*
> *I don't hold on to anything, don't reject anything;*
> *nowhere an obstacle or conflict.*
> *Who cares about wealth and honor?*
> *Even the poorest thing shines.*
> *My miraculous power and spiritual activity:*
> *drawing water and carrying wood.*

Ultimately, nothing in this life is "commonplace," nothing is "in between." The threads that join your every act, your every thought, are infinite. All paths of mastery eventually merge.

Chapter 14

Packing for the Journey

Enough delay. It's time to get packed and get on the path. Maybe you're starting something new, a journey into an unfamiliar realm of mastery. Maybe you've decided to get on the path, at long last, in some old skill you've been dabbling in, obsessing over, or hacking at for months or years. Or maybe you've vowed to treat your entire life, to the best of your ability, as a process of mastery.

In any case, here's a checklist of what you'll be taking along from this guidebook, followed by a few parting gifts for your knapsack to make your journey more pleasant and to use on those inevitable occasions when the path seems steep and rocky and hard to bear. Start with the checklist. Take a look at these items as you put them in your traveling bag and refer back to them at any time during your trip.

Now for a few parting gifts. The following mind-body exercises are taken from Leonard Energy Training (LET), a discipline inspired by my practice of aikido. This work has been introduced, since 1973, to around 50,000 people, ranging from athletes to corporate executives to couples interested in improving their relationships. LET uses the body as a metaphor for the way you deal with the problems of daily life, and as a learning facility for changing the way you deal with those problems, whether the problems are physical, mental, or emotional. It can be especially useful for those embarked on the journey of mastery.

Balancing and centering. To be balanced means that the weight of your body is distributed evenly, right and left, forward and back, all the way from the head to the toes. To be centered means that bodily awareness is concentrated in the center of the abdomen rather than, say, the head or shoulders, and that movement is initiated from this center. The important point to bear in mind here is that to be psychologically balanced and centered depends to a great extent on being physically balanced and centered.

For most of us top-heavy, forward-pushing Westerners, something as simple as focusing our attention on the abdomen can sometimes bring extraordinary results. During a moment of crisis, for example, just touching yourself lightly at the physical center (a point in the abdomen an inch or two below the navel) can significantly alter your attitude and your ability to deal with whatever situation you face. Try this: stand normally and draw your attention to the top of your body by tapping yourself a couple of times on the forehead. Then have a partner push you from behind at the shoulder blades just hard enough to make you lose your balance and take a step forward. Next, stand exactly the same way and draw your attention to your center by tapping yourself a couple of times about an inch or two below the navel. Then have your partner push you exactly the same way with exactly the same force as before. Most people find they are more stable with their attention on their centers.

You'll need someone to read these instructions

while one or more people go through the full balancing and centering procedure. Read slowly and clearly, pausing for a while wherever there are ellipses.

"Please stand with your feet slightly farther apart than your shoulders, eyes open, knees not locked and not bent, trunk upright, arms relaxed by your sides. . . . Now take the fingers of your right hand and touch them to a spot an inch or two below your navel. Press in firmly toward the center of your abdomen. . . . Now drop your right hand to your side. . . . Breathe normally. Let the breath move downward through your body as if it were going directly to your center. Let your abdomen expand with the incoming breath, from the center outward to the front, to the rear, to the sides of the pelvis, and to the floor of the pelvis. . . .

"As your breathing continues in a relaxed manner, lift your arms in front of you, with the wrists entirely limp. Shake your hands so hard that your entire body vibrates. . . . Now lower your arms slowly to your sides. As soon as they touch your legs, let them start rising very slowly, directly in front of you, just as if you were standing up to your neck in warm salt water and as if your arms were floating up to the surface. As the arms rise, lower your body by bending the knees slightly. Let your hands hang loosely, palms down, just as they would if floating in salt water. Keep the trunk upright. When your arms reach the horizontal, put the palms forward into the position you would use if gently pushing a beach ball on the surface of the water—shoulders relaxed. Now sweep your arms from left to right and right to left as if you could sense or 'see' things around you through your open palms. . . .

"Shake out your hands and repeat the process. Lower your arms to your sides and let them float up again. As the arms rise, the body lowers slightly. Knees bent, trunk upright. Now put the palms forward and sweep your arms from side to side as if sensing the world through your palms. . . .

"All right. Drop your hands, and this time leave them hanging by your sides naturally, in a totally relaxed manner. . . . Close your eyes. Knees not locked and not bent. Now check to see if your weight is distributed evenly between your right and left foot. Shift your weight very slightly from side to side, fine-tuning your balance. . . . Now check to see that your weight is balanced evenly between the heels and balls of your feet. . . . Knees not locked and not bent. . . . Please leave your eyes closed and shift to a more comfortable position any time you wish. . . . Now move your head forward and backward to find the point at which it can be balanced upright on your spine with the least muscular effort. Be sensitive, as if you were fine-tuning a distant station on your radio. . . .

"Take a moment to relax your jaw . . . your tongue . . . the muscles around your eyes . . . your forehead, temples, scalp . . . the back of your neck. . . .

"Now, with a sharp inhalation of breath, raise and tighten your shoulders. . . . As you exhale, let your shoulders drop. They aren't slumping forward, but melting straight downward, like soft, warm chocolate. With each outgoing breath, let them melt a little farther. . . . Let that same melting sensation move down your arms, down to your hands. Feel your hands become heavy and warm. . . . Let the feeling of melting move down your shoulder blades . . . your rib cage, front, back, and sides . . . down to your diaphragm. . . . Let all of your internal organs rest, relax, soften. . . . And now the lower pelvic region; let that relax also. Release all tension. With each outgoing breath, let go a bit more. . . . Let the melting, relaxing sensation move down your legs to your feet. . . . Feel your feet warming the floor and the floor warming your feet. Sense the secure embrace of gravity that holds you to the earth and holds the earth to you. . . .

"Now consider the back half of your body. What if you could sense what is behind you? What would that be like? What if you had sensors, or 'eyes,' in the small of your back? . . . At the back of your neck?

. . . At the back of your knees? . . . At the back of your heels? . . . With your eyes closed, can you get the general *feel* of what is behind you? . . .

"Now send a beam of awareness throughout your entire body, seeking out any area that might be tense or rigid or numb. Just illuminate that area; focus on it. Sometimes awareness alone takes care of these problems. . . .

"Once more, concentrate on your breathing. . . . Be aware of the rhythm. . . . Now, in synchrony with an incoming breath, let your eyes open. Don't look at any one thing in particular. Just let the world come in. . . . With eyes soft and relaxed, walk around slowly, maintaining the relaxed and balanced state you've achieved. . . . Let your physical center be a center of awareness. . . . Ask yourself if things look and feel different to you after this exercise."

Once you've gone through the balancing and centering procedure a few times, you'll find that you can recreate it rather quickly—in as little as a few seconds, in fact. To repeat the most important point: the body can be considered a metaphor for everything else. Your relationships, your work, your chores, your entire life can be centered and balanced.

Returning to center. There will be moments on the path, no matter how skillful and well-balanced you might be, when you'll be knocked off center. But don't despair; you can practice for this eventuality. And if you stay aware, it's possible to return to the balanced and centered state at an even deeper level. Here are two ways to practice regaining your center.

1. Stand with eyes closed; balance and center yourself. Then, with knees bent, lean over from the waist. Let your arms hang down toward the floor. When you've become accustomed to this position, straighten up rather suddenly and immediately open your eyes. Fully experience your sense of disorientation; don't struggle forcibly to regain your composure. Rather than that, touch your center with one hand and settle down into a balanced and centered state. Be aware of what happens during the process. Does the condition of being centered and balanced seem somehow deeper and more powerful after having been momentarily lost?

2. Go through your balancing and centering procedure while standing with eyes open. Leaving the eyes open, spin several times to the left, then to the right—just enough to become slightly dizzy. Don't overdo it. Then stop spinning, touch your center, and return to the balanced and centered state with increased awareness of the soles of your feet. Again, be aware of what goes on during the process of regaining center.

Remember the feeling of these two exercises when

you're knocked off center either physically or psychologically.

Gaining energy from unexpected blows. No matter how well we plan it, life is bound to include sudden shocks—physical or psychological misfortunes that come when we least expect them. The unexpected blow can range from the loss of a favorite piece of jewelry to the loss of a loved one, from being fired to having your mate leave you. Sometimes we struggle blindly against such misfortunes, which only gives them additional power over our lives. Sometimes we steel ourselves and deny the pain and shock, which tends to block *all* of our feelings and makes it impossible to gain anything positive from the experience. Sometimes we waste our time by doing nothing but bemoaning our ill fortune. Here's a different approach, a way to gain energy from even a serious blow. You might call it taking the hit as a gift.

Have someone stand silently behind you. With eyes open, balance and center yourself. When you're ready, hold your arms out to the sides at forty-five degree angles. This is the signal for the person behind you to quietly walk up and grab one of your wrists with just enough impact to startle you; that is, to simulate an unexpected blow. Don't struggle against the grab or try to pretend you weren't upset. Instead, become fully aware of just how the grab affected you. Describe it aloud, as specifically as possible. (For example, "My heart seemed to jump up into my throat" or "My eyes blinked and something like an electric current seemed to shoot up my left arm.") As your partner continues to hold your wrist firmly, go on describing your sensations. Hold nothing back; it's important here and in the case of real blows to face your situation squarely, and to experience and acknowledge your feelings about it.

Once you've done this, lower your body by bending your knees slightly and return to a balanced and centered state, while your partner continues to hold your wrist. Consider the possibility that the wrist grab actually adds energy to your system, and that you can use that energy to deal with your current situation, maybe with plenty left over. Breathe deeply. Let the feeling of arousal and clarity, triggered by the release of adrenaline into your bloodstream, course freely through your entire being. Have your partner release your wrist. Walk around expansively. Consider the possibility that any sudden misfortune that befalls you during your journey can be converted to positive energy.

An introduction to ki. It's called ki in Japanese, ch'i in Chinese, pneuma in Greek, prana in Sanskrit, and, you might say, "the Force" in the Star Wars trilogy. In the ancient tradition, the word comes from the notion of breath, and is considered the fundamental energy of the universe that connects all things and undergirds all creative action. The Eastern martial arts share a common faith in this energy. By somehow controlling its flow in one's own body or projecting it toward external objects, the martial artist can supposedly achieve extraordinary powers. Legends abound of masters who can stop an opponent in his tracks from halfway across a room, or even throw him head over heels. Karate practitioners generally claim that ki, even more than muscular strength, makes it possible for them to break boards or concrete blocks.

Thus far, ki has proved difficult to measure, and skeptics tend to attribute its powers to suggestion, a sort of dynamic placebo effect. To the pragmatist, this distinction is unimportant. As a practitioner of aikido, an art in which ki plays an especially important role, I've generally found a strong correlation between my perception of personal ki and the effectiveness of my techniques (see Key Four: Intentionality, page 89). The idea of ki can offer the untrained person an effective way of gaining a sensation of increased power along with relaxation, especially during times of fatigue and stress, and thus is a useful item to pack for your journey.

Here's an exercise designed to demonstrate the power that can come from visualizing ki. Because the exercise involves rising from sitting to standing with a partner trying to hold you down, don't attempt it if you have any problems with your knees, back, or abdomen.

Sit in an armless, straight-backed chair with your hands on your knees. Try rising to a standing position several times, noting just how you do it. Now have your partner put his or her hands on your shoulders and push down. Using the same motions as before, try to rise with muscular force, pushing upward against the downward pressure of your partner's hands. Have your partner press down just hard enough to make it difficult for you to get up.

Have your partner remove his or her hands. Remaining seated, take a few moments to relax. Let go all the tension in your chest and shoulders. Feel your feet making a firm connection with the floor. Place the palm of your left hand on your abdomen and feel it expanding with each incoming breath. Put your left hand on your knee and continue breathing in the same way.

Now imagine a radiant ball of ki energy about the size of a grapefruit in the center of your abdomen. Imagine that it expands and contracts with each breath. Make this ball of ki the center of your attention. Have your partner push down on your shoulders again, with the same amount of pressure as before. This time don't pay any attention to the pressure. Assume the ball of ki will provide the power you'll need to stand. Keeping your attention on the ki in your abdomen, rise to a standing position using the same physical motions as before.

Notice the difference between the two experiences. Whether the ki is "real" or only a psychological aid is perhaps less important than the results you achieve. In any case, you didn't *create* the ki. According to the best thinking on this subject, the ki was already there. It's everywhere.

Relaxing for power. The word power springs from French and Latin roots meaning "to be able." At best, this ableness applies not to achieving dominance over other people but to realizing your own potential for mastery. Power, in any case, is closely allied with relaxation. Just as a tense muscle loses in strength, so a rigid, tense, and overbearing attitude eventually fails.

Start by standing and extending one arm to a horizontal position directly in front of you. Either arm will do, but let's say it's the right arm this time. The hand should be open with the fingers spread and the thumb pointing straight up. Have a partner stand at the right of your arm and bend it at the elbow by pressing up at your wrist and down at your elbow. Don't resist. Note that this exercise involves bending the arm at the elbow, not the shoulder.

Now that your partner has practiced bending your arm without any resistance on your part, you'll try two radically different ways of making your arm strong and resilient. After each of these, your partner will attempt to bend your arm at the elbow, adding force gradually. Your partner should not add so much force that a struggle ensues. Bear in mind that this isn't a contest but rather a comparison of two different ways of being powerful. The point is to see how much effort is required to keep the arm straight under pressure.

THE FIRST WAY: Hold your arm rigidly straight. Use your muscles to keep your arm from being bent. Have your partner gradually apply force in an attempt to bend your arm. It might bend or it might not. In either case, note how much effort you exerted in the process. Perhaps even more important, note how you feel about this experience.

THE SECOND WAY: Let your arm rise to the same horizontal position as before. This time, sense the aliveness of your arm and the energy flowing from your shoulder to your fingertips. Now visualize or feel your arm as part of a powerful laser beam that extends out past your fingertips, through any walls or other objects in front of you, across the horizon and to the ends of the universe. This beam is larger in diameter than your arm, and your arm is an integral part of it. Think of the beam as ki if you wish. Your arm is not rigid or tense. In fact, it's quite relaxed. But remember: being relaxed is *not* being limp. Your arm is full of life and energy. If anyone tried to bend your arm, the beam would become even more powerful and penetrating, and your arm, without effort, would also become more powerful.

Now have your partner gradually apply exactly the same amount of force as before in an attempt to bend your arm. Note how much effort you exerted in this case. How do you feel about the experience?

An overwhelming majority of people who have tried this exercise find the second way, the "energy arm," far more powerful and resilient than the first way, the "resistance arm." Electromyographic measurements of the electrical activity in the muscles indicate that this subjective judgement is correct. The energy arm might give a little but is far less likely to collapse than the resistance arm.

The implications for physical performance are obvious: relaxation is essential for the full expression of power. If we take the body as a metaphor for everything else in our lives, the implications are even more significant. Just think what kind of world it would be if we all realized that we could be powerful in everything we do without being tense and rigid.

These parting gifts, I hope, will be of use to you on your journey of mastery, as will the other information provided in this book. At this moment, however, I am struck by the insignificance of anything I or anyone else could give you compared with what you already have. You are the culmination of an extravagant evolutionary journey. Your DNA contains more information than all of the libraries in the world; information that goes back to the beginnings of life itself. In potentia, you are the most formidable all-around athlete who has ever roamed this planet. Many creatures possess more highly specialized sense organs, but no total sensorium is so well equipped and integrated as is yours. (The unaided human eye can detect a single quantum of light—the smallest amount possible—and discern more than ten million colors.) Your brain is the most complex entity in the known universe; its billions of twinkling neurons interact in ways so multitudinous and multifarious as to dwarf the capacity of any computer ever yet devised or even imagined. The best way to describe your total creative capacity is to say that for all practical purposes it is infinite.

Whatever your age, your upbringing, or your education, what you are made of is mostly unused potential. It is your evolutionary destiny to use what is unused, to learn and keep on learning for as long as you live. To choose this destiny, to walk the path of mastery, isn't always easy, but it is the ultimate human adventure. Destinations will appear in the distance, will be achieved and left behind, and still the path will continue. It will never end.

How to begin the journey? You need only to take the first step. When? There's always now.

The Master and the Fool

"I want you to tell me how I can be a learner."

It was not so much a query as a demand, almost a threat. He was a mountain man, with the long black hair, bold moustache and rough-hewn clothing of a nineteenth-century outlaw, one of a breed that lived illegally in the rugged hills of the Los Padres National Wilderness Area along the Big Sur coast of California—a place of buzzards and hawks, mountain lions and wild boar. Having just turned in the final proofs of a book on education (it was in the late 1960s), I had driven four hours south from San Francisco for a weekend of relaxation at Esalen Institute.

As I approached the lodge—a rustic building built at the edge of the Pacific on one of the few areas of flat land between the sea and the mountains of the Los Padres—I heard the sound of conga drums. Inside, the mountain man was sitting at one of the

169

drums, surrounded by eight other people, each also at a drum. He was apparently giving an informal lesson to whoever cared to participate. One of the drums was unoccupied. I pulled up to the unoccupied drum and joined the others, following the instruction as well as I could. When the session ended I started to walk away, but the mountain man came after me, grasped my shoulder, and fixed me with a significant look.

"Man," he said, "you are a *learner*."

I stood there speechless. I'd never met this person, and he certainly had no idea I had just finished a book about learning. My conservative city garb had probably led him to think that I was a complete novice at the conga drum, the instrument of choice of the counterculture, and thus he must have been impressed by my seemingly rapid progress. Still, I was so pleased by his words that I didn't inform him I'd played before. He proceeded to tell me that he was a sculptor who worked metal with an acetylene torch, and that he was badly stuck and had been for a year; he was no longer a learner. Now he wanted me, a learner in his mind, to come up to his place in the Los Padres, look at his work, and tell him how *he* could be a learner. He was leaving right away and I could follow him in my car if I wished.

The invitation baffled me, but I realized it was a rare opportunity to visit the forbidden haunts of one of the legendary mountain men of Big Sur, so I immediately accepted. I followed his battered sedan up a steep and tortuous dirt road, then across a mountain meadow to a driveway that was nothing more than two tire tracks through a forest of live oak, madrone, and bay trees. For what seemed a long time, the car lurched and labored steeply upward, coming at last to a clearing near the top of the coast range. In the clearing stood several wooden structures: a two-room cabin, a tool shed, a crude studio for metal sculpture, and something that might have been a chicken or rabbit coop. At one point during my visit, I spotted a slim young woman with flowing blonde hair and a long dress standing like a ghost near the edge of the clearing. He never mentioned her.

The mountain man showed me into a sturdily built cabin with a large front window looking 4,000 feet down to the Pacific, now shining like a sheet of metal in the late afternoon sun. We sat and made disjointed conversation for a while. I found myself somewhat disoriented. But for the presence of several conga drums, we might have been sitting in an early nineteenth-century pioneer's cabin. It was all like a dream: the unlikely invitation, the rugged drive, the mysterious woman, the expansive gleam of the ocean through the trees.

When the mountain man announced that we would now go and look at his work so that I could tell him how to be a learner, I dumbly followed him out, having no idea of what I could possibly say that would be of any use to him. He walked me through his sculpture chronologically, showing me the point at which he had lost his creative spark, had stopped being a learner. When he finished, he fixed me with his eyes, and repeated his question one more time.

"Tell me. How can I be a learner?"

My mind went absolutely blank, and I heard myself saying, "It's simple. To be a learner, you've got to be willing to be a fool."

The mountain man nodded thoughtfully and said "thanks." There were a few more words, after which I got into my car and went back down the mountain.

Several years were to pass before I considered the possibility that my answer was anything more than a part of one of those slightly bizarre, easily forgotten sixties episodes. Still, the time did come when ideas from other places—all sorts of ideas—began to coalesce around my careless words of advice, and I began to see more than a casual relationship between learning and the willingness to be foolish, between the master and the fool. By fool, to be clear, I don't mean a stupid, unthinking person, but one with the spirit of the medieval fool, the court jester, the carefree fool in the tarot deck who bears the awesome number zero, signifying the fertile void from which all creation springs, the state of emptiness that allows new things to come into being.

The theme of emptiness as a precondition to significant learning shows up in the familiar tale of the wise man who comes to the Zen master, haughty in his great wisdom, asking how he can become even wiser. The master simply pours tea into the wise man's cup and keeps pouring until the cup runs over and spills all over the wise man, letting him know without words that if one's cup is already full there is no space in it for anything new. Then there is the question of why young people sometimes learn new things faster than old people; why my teenage daughters, for example, learned the new dances when I didn't. Was it just because they were willing to let themselves be foolish and I was not?

Or you might take the case of an eighteen-month-old infant learning to talk. Imagine the father leaning over the crib in which his baby son is engaging in what the behaviorist B. F. Skinner calls the free operant; that is, he's simply babbling various nonsense sounds. Out of this babble comes the syllable da. What happens? Father smiles broadly, jumps up and down with joy, and shouts, "Did you hear that? My son said 'daddy.' " Of course, he didn't say "daddy." Still, nothing is much more rewarding to an eighteen-month-old infant than to see an adult smiling broadly and jumping up and down. So, the behaviorists confirm our common sense by telling us that the probability of the infant uttering the syllable da has now increased slightly.

The father continues to be delighted by da, but after a while his enthusiasm begins to wane. Finally, the infant happens to say, not da, but dada. Once again, father goes slightly crazy with joy, thus increasing the probability that his son will repeat the sound dada. Through such reinforcements and approximations, the toddler finally learns to say daddy quite well. To do so, remember, he not only has been allowed but has been encouraged to babble, to make "mistakes," to engage in approximations—in short, to be a fool.

But what if this type of permission had not been granted? Let's rerun the same scene. There's father leaning over the crib of his eighteen-month-old son. Out of the infant's babble comes the syllable da. This time, father looks down sternly and says, "No, son, that is *wrong!* The correct pronunciation is *dad-dy.* Now repeat after me: *Dad-dy. Dad-dy. Dad-dy.*"

What would happen under these circumstances? If all of the adults around an infant responded in such a manner, it's quite possible he would never learn to talk. In any case, he would be afflicted with serious speech and psychological difficulties.

If this scenario should seem extreme, consider for a moment the learnings in life you've forfeited because your parents, your peers, your school, your society, have not allowed you to be playful, free, and foolish in the learning process. How many times have you failed to try something new out of fear of being thought silly? How often have you censored your spontaneity out of fear of being thought childish? Too bad. Psychologist Abraham Maslow discovered a childlike quality (he called it a "second naivete") in people who have met an unusually high degree of their potential. Ashleigh Montagu used the term neotany (from neonate, meaning newborn) to describe geniuses such as Mozart and Einstein. What we frown at as foolish in our friends, or ourselves, we're likely to smile at as merely eccentric in a world-renowned genius, never stopping to think that the freedom to be foolish might well be one of the keys to the genius's success—or even to something as basic as learning to talk.

When Jigoro Kano, the founder of judo, was quite old and close to death, the story goes, he called his students around him and told them he wanted to be buried in his white belt. What a touching story; how humble of the world's highest-ranking judoist in his last days to ask for the emblem of the beginner! But Kano's request, I eventually realized, was less humility than realism. At the moment of death, the ultimate transformation, we are all white belts. And if death makes beginners of us, so does life—again and again. In the master's secret mirror, even at the moment of highest renown and accomplishment, there is an image of the newest student in class, eager for knowledge, willing to play the fool.

And for all who walk the path of mastery, however far that journey has progressed, Kano's request becomes a lingering question, an ever-new challenge:

Are you willing to wear your white belt?

About the Author

George Leonard is the author of nine other books, including *Education and Ecstasy* and *The Ultimate Athlete,* as well as scores of magazine articles. He served as senior editor at *Look* magazine from 1953 to 1970, where he earned an unprecedented number of national awards for education, and is currently a contributing editor for *Esquire.* He holds a third-degree black belt in the martial art of aikido and is co-owner of an aikido school in Mill Valley, California, where he lives. He also lectures widely and has developed Leonard Energy Training, a practice inspired by aikido, which he has introduced to more than forty thousand people throughout the United States and the world.